W9-CRH-942

ATLANTIC SALMON FISHING

ATLANTIC SALMON FISHING

L. James Bashline

Stackpole Books

Copyright © 1987 by L. James Bashline

Published by
STACKPOLE BOOKS
Cameron and Kelker Streets
P.O. Box 1831
Harrisburg, PA 17105

All rights reserved, including the right to reproduce this book or
portions thereof in any form or by any means, electronic or mechanical,
including photocopying, recording, or by any information storage and
retrieval system, without permission in writing from the publisher.
All inquiries should be addressed to Stackpole Books, Cameron and
Kelker Streets, P.O. Box 1831, Harrisburg, Pennsylvania 17105.

Printed in the United States of America

10 9 8 7 6 5 4 3 2 1

Library of Congress Cataloging-in-Publication Data

Bashline, L. James.
    Atlantic salmon fishing.

    Bibliography: p.
    Includes index.
    1. Atlantic salmon fishing.   I. Title.
SH685.B38   1987   799.1'755   87-9962
ISBN 0-8117-0207-3

Contents

Introduction   Atlantic Salmon – The Fish of Royalty   7

Chapter 1   What We Are Fishing For   13

Chapter 2   Where They Are Fished   23

Chapter 3   How They Are Fished   37

Chapter 4   The Rod for Atlantic Salmon   53

Chapter 5   Reels   63

Chapter 6   Lines   75

Chapter 7   Leaders   79

Chapter 8   Playing, Landing, and Releasing   87

Chapter 9   Which Fly Shall I Try First?   123

Chapter 10   Tradition Unbound   131

Chapter 11   Flies: Beyond Black and Silver   141

Chapter 12   The Dry Fly and the Salmon   153

Chapter 13   Of Guides and Sports   163

Chapter 14   What Are the Odds?   171

Chapter 15   Odds and Ends – About Gear and Such   175

Chapter 16   Caring For and Cooking the Catch   179

Chapter 17   The Areas and the Outfitters   183

Chapter 18   The State of Salmon Today   213

                 Index   218

Introduction

Atlantic Salmon— The Fish of Royalty

My mission with this book is to help the reader catch a salmon. It's fun to watch them, talk about them, aid in their well-being and restoration, and otherwise engage in talking about tackle and the places salmon frequent. But I assure you, it's far more fun to feel one on the end of your leader bolting, dashing, and jumping while making the reel whine and sending sensuous vibrations through line and rod into your hand. Yes, sensuous; I'm in love with Atlantic salmon.

With many books, the opening paragraphs are written by someone other than the author. This serves two important functions: one, it gets the author out of the embarrassing position of telling the reader how wonderful the book is going to be; and, two, it tells the reader how pleased the person writing the introduction is to have been asked to write it. There's nothing wrong with either of these. I've been thrilled to have written a couple of introductions and have had others write them for me. In this case, I wanted to write the first lines myself in an attempt to convey what, for me, is the ultimate angling experience. Besides, I had so much fun writing this book, I didn't want to share that chore with anyone.

The glorious sensation of being a part of the action is what the blood sports of fishing and hunting are about. Some hunters do not fish and some fishermen do not hunt, but the union of wild creature and human is realized in these two sports in a way that cannot be accomplished in other activities. To know a fish or game animal we must pursue it. The killing or the capture is the goal. Some may deny this, but to do so is to be less than honest. A walk in the woods with a dog while carrying a shotgun should be directed toward finding and shooting some kind of game or else it is only exercise. Carrying fishing tackle to a salmon river must be aimed at the catching of a fish. To say to yourself and others that you are merely out there to enjoy nature and its wonders may be good for the soul but it's mildly deceitful. The line between observer and participant is crossed when a fishing rod or firearm is carried.

The beginning of a book is a terrible time to introduce diversions, but I'm compelled to do so for personal and philosophical reasons. Regardless of accepted definitions, fishing and hunting are two of the select activities practiced by human beings that can legitimately be termed *sports*. With few exceptions, all other so-called sports that involve the use of a stick or a ball are not sports, they are *games*. Such games have rules that govern number of players, time frame, and how points are scored. Put another way, if a score is kept, it's a game. In the case of strenuous games in which the players are called athletes, most persons watching these events are not there to participate. While it's frequently overlooked, the Olympics are correctly labeled as games. To call someone who owns a professional baseball, football, or basketball franchise a "sportsman" is correct only if the individual fishes, hunts, sails, or canoes for pure enjoyment.

To be sure, there are laws governing where, when, and how we fish, but there are no judges (wardens) in attendance most of the time and the rules are structured to cause minimal curtailing of our pleasure. Of far more importance are the self-determined rules that an angler decides to abide by. And he observes these personal rules even when no one is watching. The thoughtful angler or hunter is a sportsman – not a game player.

In the days of government by a nobility, fishing for Atlantic salmon was considered far too important for the masses. Servants and ordinary folks ate salmon to be sure, but they were usually acquired in violation of the rules established by those who carried titles. Those who cooked and served the aristocracy got leftovers and the rest of the peasants got salmon by clandestine means. If any person was caught poaching salmon or venison, a long stay in jail, or even death, could be the punishment. Long before the medieval kings held sway, the ancient Roman Caesars were acquainted with the delights of Atlantic salmon. It has been reasonably well substantiated that the Emperor Caligula, who was fond of excess, once hosted a banquet at which two thousand salmon "cheeks" were served. The cheek of even a large salmon is but a small scallop of meat from the depression immediately below each eye. What happened to the rest of the salmon is not revealed in the chronicles – but I'll bet it didn't go to waste.

Where Caligula's salmon came from is not known either, but a good guess would be Spain. There, a few salmon still return to a handful of rivers even today, and with some nurturing they might increase in number. The Romans did some amazing things with aqueducts and highways. They also knew the value of storing and transporting meat and other perishables on ice gathered in the Alps. It's not beyond the imagination to consider that the Romans might have enjoyed some form of sport fishing for Atlantic salmon. Savoring the good life as they did, they certainly would have gotten a kick out of it.

As I grew up believing that all fishing worth the time must be done with a fly rod, to fish for Atlantic salmon one day was the absolute height of my ambition. I fished for small trout as a young kid and as quickly as I could read, began devouring any book on the subject I could beg or borrow. Most of the good reading in the thirties and forties came from the United Kingdom, and with few exceptions those tomes always had something to say about salmon. I got the distinct impression that to catch a salmon on a fly rod was almost as wonderful as being knighted. I vowed I would fish for them one day. In talking to many other anglers who had similar backgrounds, I later discovered that this desire was not an uncommon one.

Our angling heritage, much of which stems from this continent's close ties with Britain, is laced with an infatuation for Atlantic salmon. Because the fish are found here and there, the piscatorial bond is easy to understand. The British fished for trout too, thus adding to the commonality of sport. But all historical and genetic speculation aside, the Atlantic salmon puts a special gleam in the eye of anglers from any country in which the fly rod is employed. Just last season I crossed paths with two Argentinians who had journeyed from one end of the globe to the other in order to see what an Atlantic salmon looked like. They have the magnificent trout of South America at their back doors, so why did they seek *Salmo salar* in Labrador?

That question can also be asked of fly tiers in Texas who fashion Atlantic salmon flies by the dozen, carefully entering them in the clips in a Wheatley fly box. Many of these tiers won't be fishing for Atlantics this year or next, but one day they *will* fish for them. They've made the promise to themselves, and so have thousands of other anglers. A fly fisher who does not dream of casting for the king of game fish would be difficult to find.

I find any fishing preferable to no fishing. I've been lucky enough to have felt most of the world's major game-fish species on my line at one time or another. All of them have their attributes, but no single fish can possibly match the Atlantic salmon in having it all. No other fish jumps as high or runs as fast in proportion to its size. No other fish is so coveted on the dining table. No other fish takes our flies so freely and yet so guardedly when it chooses. It is *predictable* in its rises only in that it is *unpredictable*. And therein lies the charm of the Atlantic salmon.

Ernest Schweibert once made the remark, "There are no expert salmon anglers but there are some good salmon observers." I agree completely, and must add that in no way is this book designed to laud my Atlantic salmon fishing expertise. We can become highly skilled in trout or bass or a number of other species for no other reason than availability. Salmon are not always there to fish for. Our span of experience is limited considerably because they are not fulltime residents anywhere.

You will notice that the word "Atlantic" is frequently used in combination with "salmon" throughout this book. This is because I encourage it and want to make certain that nothing written on these pages will be taken as applicable to the family of Pacific salmons. They are different fish and, other than being anadromous, share few similarities with Atlantics. While I prefer fishing for Atlantic salmon and have spent far more time at it than at pursuing Pacifics, I have no intention of ever denigrating the latter. Angling for Pacific salmon is a different proposition with many avenues to explore. Chinook salmon and cohos, for example, are separate studies, as are pinks and sockeyes. To an even slightly educated palette the taste of Atlantic salmon is different from the Pacific fish. I would never be so bold as to declare one better than the other on the table – but there is a difference.

In 1985, the latest year (at this moment) for which complete figures are available, nonresident salmon anglers pumped $84 million into the Canadian economy. They caught twenty-nine percent of the Atlantic salmon taken that year. Commercial fishermen harvested seventy-one percent of the fish reported, generating only $6.5 million in revenue. These figures, taken from an independent study commissioned by the Atlantic Salmon Federation, illustrate dramatically why sport fishing for Atlantic salmon is not merely aesthetically pleasing. It brings new dollars directly to the banks of the salmon rivers. Two definitions of "bank" apply here.

The situation is improving each year in regard to better husbandry of the resource. In addition to a better appreciation of what sport fishing is worth, the artificial rearing of Atlantic salmon for commercial markets is beginning to show great promise as a means of satisfying the world demand for the flesh of this magnificent fish. Aquaculture, or "fish farming," is being done successfully in Norway and Canada, and fledgling operations are being started in half a dozen other countries. Employing penned-up saltwater lagoons, raceways, advanced methods of taking eggs, and fast-growth food formulas, propagators of salmon hold the key to supply and demand. While the true believer will insist that a pen-reared salmon cannot possibly taste as good as a wild fish, there is no evidence that many chefs or diners can tell the difference. The ultimate goal should be wild fish for the angler and domestically raised fish for the market. I believe that goal will be reached.

A word of caution is in order before you commence reading, and a flat warning is necessary if you find yourself embarking on your first Atlantic salmon adventure. If you have the soul of a fly rodder and a fisherman's heart, the chances of being mesmerized by this fish are great. Any time spent with the long rod casting for fish that will strike an artificial fly is fun—but doing it on a salmon river over these magnificent fish is captivating, and, for some, addictive. I would have difficulty surviving each winter without an Atlantic salmon "fix" and I've met several hundred fellow anglers who feel exactly the same way. Once you've experienced casting, seeing a rise, feeling the solid pull, and witnessing a living bar of silver fling itself into the morning sun, you might find other angling pleasures of secondary importance. Those of you who have been involved in this drama know how obsessive it can become.

If there must be a dedication made, I'd like to salute the Atlantic salmon. Without it this book could not exist. But special thanks must be made to Bob and Andy, "the brothers Korosec," who provided bed and board so many years ago at their cabin on the Little Southwest Miramichi. What wonderful days!

Special thanks to Duncan Barnes of *Field & Stream* magazine for allowing me to reprint portions of articles that have appeared in that magazine, and to Keith Gardner of *Fishing World* for the same favor. Thanks too, to Bob Ent of Bangor, Maine, for his artistry in tying "classics" and hairwing salmon flies for this book. J. Edson Leonard's tie of my favorite fly, the Mar Lodge, will not be returned since it's too beautiful to part with. My heartfelt gratitude to Kathy Swiderski for managing to understand my scribbling on manuscript pages. And, in the beginning and the end, there has been editor Judith Schnell of Stackpole Books, the major force in seeing this book take shape. She knew it would come together even when no one else, including me, believed it.

To list the other anglers, fly tiers, guides, and admirers of Atlantic salmon who contributed to the spiritual and physical "care and feeding" of this fishing fanatic would require several pages. I love you all.

But the most love and the most thanks must be reserved for my favorite angling partner—my patient spouse, Sylvia. She has suffered through many salmon adventures and misadventures (all the while being screamed at), shooting photos, keeping notes, keeping me out of serious trouble, and always managing to remain a lady. I love you dear, even more than I love Atlantic salmon.

Spruce Creek, Pennsylvania
March 6, 1987

1

What We Are Fishing For

The cold-blooded creatures of this world are programmed in such a way that their species "insurance policy" is built in. Unlike the majority of land-born vertebrates, the frogs, toads, salamanders, and fishes deposit hundreds and sometimes thousands of eggs each breeding season. They must. The survival rate of juvenile fish is so low that fewer than ten percent survive to continue the species. In the case of the Atlantic salmon, it's a wonder that any survive.

The adult salmon are chased on the high seas, thwarted by dams, pursued by seals, eels, birds, bears, otters, mink, and, finally, harassed by anglers when they finally make it back to the river of their birth. When the river water is usually at its lowest point in the spawning areas, making the adult fish more vulnerable to all predators, they perform their romantic duties, thus sapping most of their remaining strength. While the Atlantic salmon is capable of surviving the ordeal of mating, which its Pacific cousins are not, many of them still succumb. And then, talk about postpartum, if a sudden cold snap freezes the shallows, as frequently happens before the spawning is completed, the survivors are forced to remain under the river ice until the spring thaw. With nothing in their bellies and not much food available, it's a long cold winter indeed.

Some salmon do make it back to the ocean to wax fat once more before winter's arrival, but those that don't must run the river gauntlet again—this time drifting with the spring flood while ravenously grabbing anything that looks like food. Sad looking creatures they are: black of back and dull gray of side with heads outlandishly large for their skinny bodies, they are ghosts of the sleek, silver bullets they were the summer before. These "black salmon" or kelts can quickly be rejuvenated if they reach the salt water, but here the remaining numbers are reduced again by predators, the violence of the river, and, in many places, the angler's hook. For a few it's back to the ocean again for another session of eluding nets and seals and killer whales.

The stirrings in the salmon egg begin when the spring sun warms the nursery waters; an eye forms, now a tail, and a new fish takes shape. Its yolk sac will nourish it for a time, but as soon as the mouth and digestive tract begin to function properly, the tiny alevin will dart about looking for food. It becomes food too, for birds, eels, and other fish including trout and char, which are plentiful in many salmon rivers, as well as for young salmon parr of previous hatchings. As the alevin grows into its parr markings and spots (not much unlike a little brown trout's), it ventures into faster water and quickly learns to attack insects on the surface and in the air. It becomes an even more visible target for predators because it has become a predator itself. Some parr spend but one year feeding in their natal river before heading for the ocean, but the vast majority must face the river's risks for two and occasionally three or four years. The period varies with rivers, watersheds, and races of salmon. It is yet another of nature's built-in systems of providing more than necessary to guarantee the continuation of the species.

During a salmon's life, several magic times occur that totally confound scientific deduction. One of these takes place on a spring day when the ice is gone, water temperature is suitable, and the ocean's call is heard. What that "call" consists of can be romantically phrased in many ways and biologically explained until total confusion sets in. The fact is, we don't know why, but immediately prior to its downstream trip, the parr becomes a *smolt*—a silvery pocket edition of the big salmon it will ultimately become. It has long been a popular theory that the salt water brings on the silvery sheen that practically all ocean feeders wear, but the salmon smolt takes on this new-coin gleam before reaching the salt. When these adolescents are ready to begin their first ocean feeding period, like teenagers everywhere anticipating a big adventure, they dash about wildly.

Since the small fish that have been feeding as parr, and now as smolts of eight to twelve inches, are capable of taking larger prey, it has always seemed strange to me that more smolts are not caught by anglers who are on the rivers in late spring. Occasionally some are caught by sea-trout anglers in the estuaries, but why not more in the streams? During thirty years of Atlantic salmon fishing I have yet to catch one and have only seen two actually caught on flies. Some are caught of course, but even guides and

A typical Atlantic salmon parr. These little fish will strike full-size salmon flies with gusto, emulating their larger relatives. At times their frequent strikes become a nuisance. Careful release is called for here—these juveniles will be grilse two years hence.

fishermen who live by salmon rivers usually count their lifetime smolt catches on one hand. In conversations with dozens of highly experienced salmon anglers, the same consensus prevails: very few if any smolts have been caught. Even Lee Wulff, the guru of North American Atlantic salmon anglers, can recall catching a half dozen at the most. And Lee has fished more than a few salmon rivers when smolt runs were probably ten times heavier than they are today. Says Lee, "I believe that the bulk of the smolt leave the rivers well before the first large salmon enter from the sea. Therefore, our chances of catching them are reduced. In addition, the well-seasoned salmon angler learns to control his reflexes and comes back hard only on strikes which are obviously salmon. One learns not to jerk on parr bumps and even on sizable trout of ten inches or a foot long. Some of these strikes could be smolt, but we'll never know."

One spring morning during the early sixties while I was searching for bear sign along the northwest Miramichi, one of that river's tributaries was full of darting smolts. There were thousands of them milling about. The next day, it was as if the river had gone dead. Not a smolt was seen in the immediate pools, nor were any seen the next week on the entire length of the river. As I recall, this was about mid-May. That mysterious call of the sea came suddenly and the fish responded en masse. Another of the salmon's unexplained mysteries.

We now know that the majority of the salmon spawned in the rivers that flow into the Atlantic Ocean from two continents and several island nations end up at the same feeding grounds in the Davis Strait, but not much else has been substantiated. The primary meals appear to consist of capelin, prawns, and assorted baitfish, but the travels of salmon while feeding are not well recorded. Do they feed near the surface, the middle depths, or near the bottom? Do they travel in large schools or "wolf pack" bands as Pacific salmon sometimes do? Is their route from river to feeding area direct, or are there way stations along the trail? Someday we may unravel these puzzles, and others, but in the meantime, most of us who love this fish and its pursuit find some pleasure in our ignorance. This business of our not knowing it all is a large part of the salmon's intrigue. Isn't the dressing gown-covered female form the more exciting because of what's not known? (I hasten to point out that that's not a sexist remark — conversely, we all know proper ladies who enjoy watching athletes in tight-fitting uniforms, even though they don't care much about the outcome of the game.)

In direct contrast to the slow growth of the salmon from egg through parr to smolt stage in the fresh water, the young salmon acquires weight and length rapidly in the salt. Its metabolic rate must make an amazing switch, since ten-inch salmon can weigh five or five-and-a-half pounds after a thirteen- or fourteen-month feeding session. The fish in this size range are usually termed grilse and today form the bulk of the rod-and-reel catch on many rivers. Nailing down the definition of a grilse is like asking a politician a direct question: you'll get answers but they do little to illuminate the issue.

There is general agreement, on most rivers and among those with a few seasons on

This high-jumping grilse is a full four feet out of the water. Not a record jump by any means, because Atlantic salmon have been observed leaping vertically over seven feet!

Author with an exceptionally heavy grilse. Note that the tail rays are beginning to develop, as is the kype on the lower jaw.

their waders, that a grilse is a salmon that has spent but one season feeding in salt water. But the problem of definition is compounded by the fact that some grilse spend a bit more and some a bit less than the usual thirteen months in the brine. Feeding time is a major factor in deciding how much a grilse will weigh or how long it will be. In addition, certain races of fish and some specific individuals will grow faster or slower. I've seen grilse that weighed less than two-and-a-half pounds and some that have weighed nearly seven. There are rivers where grilse don't appear to be grilse at all. They don't weigh a great deal more than five pounds but display larger head bones and rather well-defined tail rays that are the ordinary signs of an adult salmon.

Okay, then, what's an adult salmon? An adult Atlantic salmon, by the yardstick I choose to use, is one that has developed sufficiently so that its tail rays are solid enough for the fish to be easily picked up by the "wrist," just forward of the tail itself. With the majority of salmon, this criterion will apply to fish of seven pounds or more. Put another way, any fish that weighs in excess of seven pounds has probably fed more than thirteen months in the salt.

In most salmon rivers of North America, the adult salmon and grilse begin to reenter their natal rivers about the time the snow melt is nearly gone. The lack of a turbulent flow may or may not trigger the actual ascent; we know that in other countries where Atlantic salmon exist, there may be no snow of a winter. A more likely signal is the increase in the daylight period. This, combined with the expansion of the egg mass in the females and the milt sacs of the males, pressure the fish to make their move from salt to sweet water. And here again, what we do not know about the comings and goings of this marvelous game fish is at once of great concern and of little consequence. We want to know, but, childlike, we're happy not knowing it all. It's delightful to be hoodwinked by the sleight-of-hand artist. The magic makes children laugh and gasp. And so it is with salmon fishers.

The more southern the latitude, the earlier the fish return to the rivers. In Maine, for example, salmon frequently show up in early May and have been caught even earlier. The middle of June sees them in New Brunswick and just a bit later in Newfoundland. The first serious runs come during the first week of July on Quebec's north shore of the St. Lawrence. And so it goes, a week or two later as one travels up the coast of Labrador and around the corner into Ungava Bay. I believe it's the light, or photo period, that brings them back on schedule, but other factors can advance or delay the process slightly. A late spring with too much ice, abnormally low water, or a sudden and prolonged rise in air temperature can all affect when salmon will enter a river. But come they will, and the arrival date won't vary by many days. *How* they get back is the next in our series of conundrums.

There is considerable evidence to suggest that salmon are gregarious and tend generally to stick together in "river families" while feeding in the ocean. Unfortunately, if a netter happens to set his trap just right, an entire breeding population, or the best part of it, could be eliminated in one swoop on the high seas. Barring such an event, the fish from a particular river seem to decide collectively when it's time to head for home. There has been much learned speculation about how they navigate across vast tracts of dark ocean water. Some fish don't have to travel far to get back from that magic spot off Greenland, but others must travel two thousand miles and more. There are no road maps.

Some fanciful ideas cropped up in the British Isles a few centuries ago concerning this navigational feat. Some believed that salmon used the stars as directional guide posts, while others thought that certain physical signs such as reefs, underwater ridges, and the like were the helpers. Another theory held that certain birds such as gulls and albatrosses "guided" the salmon back to the shore. Well, maybe, but I choose to believe that the ocean currents, which are controlled in part by the earth's inner gravitational force, and the rotation of the sphere itself create the invisible channels by which the salmon find home again—or very close to it.

Once the fish gets within a day's swimming of home, more or less, there can be little dispute about what leads the way. It's the salmon's nose. It smells the river being searched for. Every river has its individual aroma, a complex blend of chemicals, derived from rock and soil make-up, botanicals, and other life forms. Experimental plugging of fishes' nostrils has proven that the hampered fish are disoriented and simply don't know which river to enter. Removal of the plugs gets the salmon right back on track. Salmon trapped a few miles away from *their* river and then released will make a beeline for the familiar campground in a hurry. Dumping various dyes of an inert nature doesn't fool them, but adding different flavors (chemicals) to the water can stop migrating fish dead in their wake.

Once the salmon find *their* river mouth, they may or may not enter quickly. The flow of the water has to be to their liking, and the pushing action of the tide just right. Salmon usually enter a river on the high tide, but they've been observed making a dash for it at all times. I've seen pods of salmon under the bridge at Red Bank, New Brunswick, wait for several days before a tide to their liking swept them into the Little Southwest Miramichi. Conversely, I've seen fish in the same location come in from the sea, mill about for a few hours, and quickly dash upstream with little fanfare. Most often they time their freshwater entry with a tide that occurs during the dark hours, making the observation of this movement a rare event. But as we've already noted, and will many more times before this book is concluded, salmon can be counted on to break every rule man has drawn up for them.

The anadromous fishes, of which the salmon is the most perfect example, manage to achieve a physiological transformation that few other creatures are capable of. They can switch the life support system from breathing salt water to fresh water in a matter of minutes, and perhaps seconds. I had to add "seconds," because I've hooked fish in totally fresh water locations and had them race headlong back into salt water, or at least

Removing scales from a fresh salmon for aging. Examining scales under magnification is not a foolproof way of determining a salmon's birthday, but it's much quicker than a complete dissection.

into a brackish blend of salt and fresh, and continue the battle. In these situations I never noticed the slightest hesitation or gasping for breath. A reverse happening was related to me by an angler on the Hunt River in Labrador. He hooked a fish quite by accident in the salt, and it proceeded to run upstream and actually leap a low falls to enter fresh water.

Under normal circumstances a pod of salmon will move together from salt to fresh after a half day of "testing" and tasting the sweet smell of home. I don't believe that salmon actually think, but they certainly seem to get pretty excited about the experience of being back in the river again. At the first of the freshwater pools, they frequently do a lot of dashing about and leaping clear of the water in a teenage manner. It appears that they just feel good about the whole thing. They're seeing their buddies again, and, of course, romance is in the offing. Please don't find me guilty of anthropomorphism; I don't believe in that nonsense. But on the other hand, it's difficult for us humans to "think" in fish language. So we do the best we can.

In this fisherman's look at the salmon's life history, I've made no attempt to delve deeply into weighty piscatorial problems. I will leave that to the scientists and ichthyologists who should properly attend to such matters. I am far more interested in fishing for *Salmo salar*, and I suspect most readers are too. It serves us well to know more about our quarry, and elsewhere in this book I'll suggest some reading material of a more technical nature. But for now, let's get on with the fishing, the flies, and the fun of chasing this most fascinating creature.

2

Where They Are Fished

There are no ugly salmon rivers. From Iceland's moonscape settings to the thickest conifer forests of the Canadian maritimes, all salmon rivers feature pools and riffles, runs and glides, that beckon as seductively as the flashing eyes of a veiled belly dancer. To continue the metaphor, once the veil is removed, the fly fisherman who has tossed his feathers only at trout will discover that the best-looking spots may not appeal to the Atlantic salmon. Oh, the water chosen could hold salmon, but if brook trout share the habitat, as they frequently do, those will be the fish that will be caught. The good trout fisherman learns to "think" like a trout, and so must the salmon angler try to think like the salmon. Until a better theory comes along, I'm prepared to believe that salmon don't think at all. They don't *act*—they *react*.

After seeing a few thousand salmon come to my flies and the flies of others, I firmly believe that they don't premeditate the rise or the strike. If the fly drifts by in an attitude that appeals to them—*bam!*—they grab it before any thought process has a chance to work, even if it could. We'll get into this apparent hocus-pocus a bit later, but to make a rise occur, it follows that one must be casting to a place where the salmon are or might be.

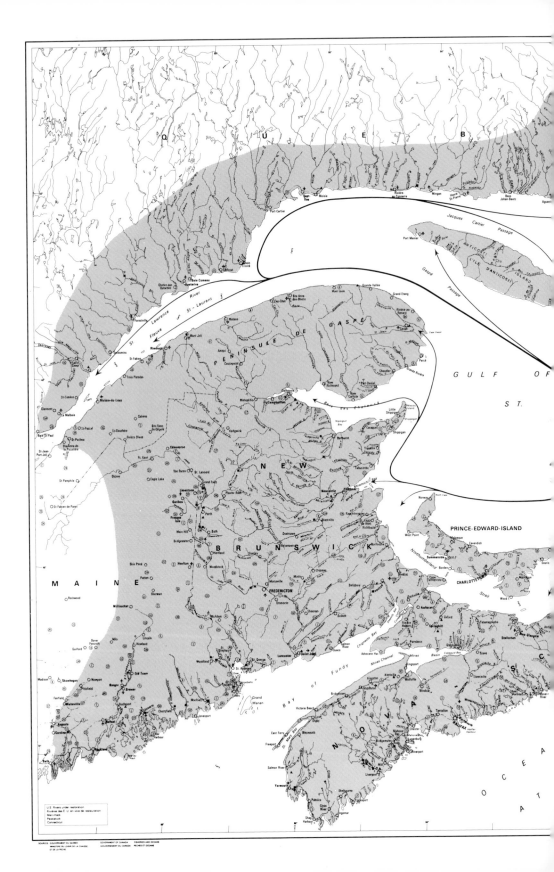

U.S. Rivers under restoration
Rivières des E. U. en voie de restauration
Merrimack
Pawcatuck
Connecticut

SOURCES: GOUVERNEMENT DU QUÉBEC   GOVERNMENT OF CANADA   FISHERIES AND OCEANS
MINISTÈRE DU LOISIR DE LA CHASSE   GOUVERNEMENT DU CANADA   PÊCHES ET OCÉANS
ET DE LA PÊCHE

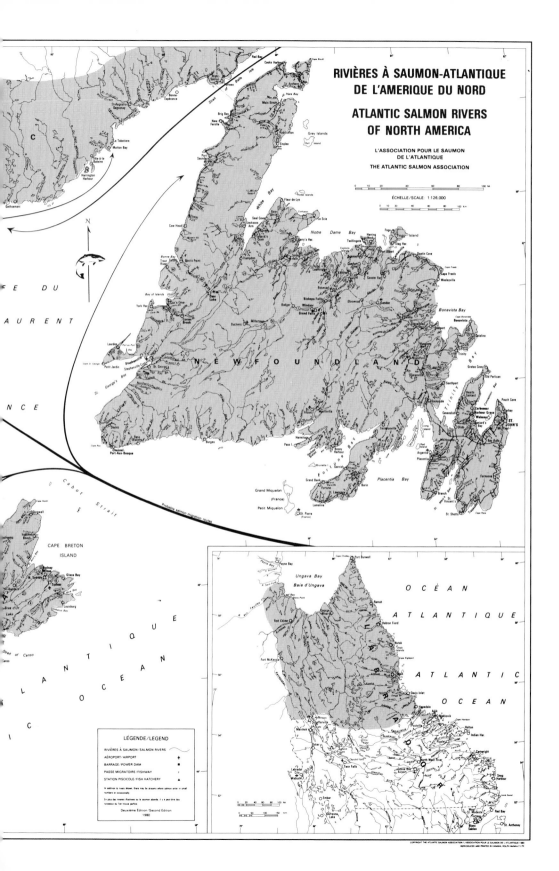

RIVIÈRES À SAUMON-ATLANTIQUE
DE L'AMERIQUE DU NORD

ATLANTIC SALMON RIVERS
OF NORTH AMERICA

L'ASSOCIATION POUR LE SAUMON
DE L'ATLANTIQUE

THE ATLANTIC SALMON ASSOCIATION

ÉCHELLE/SCALE: 1:126,000

LÉGENDE/LEGEND

RIVIÈRES À SAUMON/SALMON RIVERS

AÉROPORT/AIRPORT

BARRAGE/POWER DAM

PASSE MIGRATOIRE/FISHWAY

STATION PISCICOLE/FISH HATCHERY

In addition to rivers shown, there may be streams where salmon arise in small numbers or occasionally.

En plus des rivières illustrées où le saumon abonde, il y a peut-être des ruisseaux où l'on trouve parfois.

Deuxième Édition/Second Edition
1980

COPYRIGHT THE ATLANTIC SALMON ASSOCIATION/L'ASSOCIATION POUR LE SAUMON DE L'ATLANTIQUE 1980
REPRODUCED AND PRINTED IN CANADA, ROLPH McNALLY LTD.

Inuit guide Conluci Snowball nets a twenty-pound George River salmon for the author. The fish was hooked directly above the little section of broken water in the center of the photo.

The experienced salmoneer develops an instinctive radar system that guides the casting arm in the direction of a likely salmon "lie." The surface velocity, the presence of a certain size boulder or rock ledge, turbulent water above or below the supposed holding position, can all be factors. Then again, none of the traditional "right" things may be present. But the salmon may still be there, and the reason, if searched for, can usually be explained to the angler's satisfaction. The conclusion may not be the correct one, but if the fish are there, who cares?

There are two typical locations I would never pass up if I found myself on a strange river. The first is a slick glide at the end of a long, still piece of water that slides into severe white water or a falls. The second is below a falls or series of rapids where a deep channel slowly fans into a reasonably quiet area. The first selection is promising, because after a fish has put forth a good measure of effort to battle a frothy obstacle, it seeks some rest. But being the strong fish it is, the salmon enjoys the current when fresh from the sea and doesn't particularly like calm water. Where it spills over a slick glide, the water appears to be zipping along. The trout angler would think it's much too fast there for a good drift of a wet fly, and a dry fly would be out of the question. However, as fast as the water seems to be moving, it's not quite so fast on the bottom where the salmon clings. With minimal tail wagging, the salmon can hold its position well and will astound the novice salmon watcher with its speed and accuracy in rising for a skimming wet fly (if struck by the notion).

A slick deep channel below a falls or rocky battery is a reverse situation. Here, the salmon seem to realize that breaching what's ahead is going to take some doing. They may have approached the fast water or falls a time or two and decided to rest again before having another go at it. There may be fish strung along the deep channel to the point where the dead water begins again. If there are car-size boulders in this channel, it's almost a sure bet that the largest fish in the pool will find them attractive. And here's another of those wonderful salmon mysteries. The precise size of the boulders they enjoy being close to is an important factor in predicting where a salmon might be in a given river. The size of the boulder is not constant in terms of a specific river but constant rather in the way the water flows over or beside it.

A perfect example of this is the landmark rock at a place called the "Bathtub" on Labrador's lower Eagle River. The exposed portion of the Bathtub Rock is about the size of a Volkswagen. How big it really is cannot be stated, because to my knowledge, no one has ever donned a wet suit to find out. At normal flow there is a heavy current sweeping the far side (non-fishing side), which comes directly from a menacing series of rapids. It's a veritable cauldron of frothy water lashing in all directions as the flow is fractured by a series of ledges and even larger boulders. Charging through this obstacle requires considerable energy on the salmon's part. The fish wait below it until the spirit moves them properly. The near side of the Bathtub Rock has strong current too, but not quite so strong as the other side. As regular as the sun rises, salmon return to this

Sea lice cling to bright salmon for three or four days after they enter fresh water. When you catch a salmon with these lice attached, it's a sure bet the fish isn't long out of the ocean.

spot year after year and take up positions so tight to the rock that they seem to be hugging it. My guess is that in spite of the churning that's going on at the surface, the big rock checks the flow in such a way that at about the six- or seven-foot depth, the current is just right for holding position. When bright salmon are in the river, this spot will produce fish after fish if the angler casts his fly to the upstream side of the rock and allows it to skim past the near side in a looping arc.

But there's a Catch-22 in this procedure. The fly must swing past the rock at a slightly slower speed than that of the current. A random cast and haphazard drift won't work most of the time. The cast must be well above the holding position and the line mended with the tip time after time to keep the fly in the productive water for as long as possible. If this is accomplished, the angler is rewarded with a boiling strike that requires no hook-setting. The fish appear to bolt straight from the rock itself.

Special note: If you find yourself on the lower Eagle at Peter Paor's camp, try to fish the Bathtub in waders rather than from a boat. First, you'll get more strikes while standing on the slim rock ledge, an easy thirty-foot cast away; and second, it's exciting as hell to have a salmon jump directly under your rod tip, which they frequently do at this spot.

Another equally famous rock, although a much smaller one, is about in the middle of a pool named Steady on the Gros Mecatina on Quebec's north shore of the St. Lawrence. Without any equivocation whatsoever, this is my favorite salmon pool in the entire world. It is the spot where I once hooked and lost nine fish in less than twenty minutes before discovering that there was no point or barb on my hook. A stupid oversight on my part, not to check after the first loss, but memorable just the same. It is also the pool where I watched Sylvia land her first adult salmon, a bright cockfish of eighteen pounds that ran the reel to the spool before stopping to rest. And it was again and again the pool where first-timers hooked and landed their first salmon ever . . . a wonderful vicarious thrill that I fully enjoy as much as anything in this world. But the rock; ah, yes.

This particular rock is no larger than a clothes dryer and about the same shape. The current is not severe on either side of it, and in fact there isn't much current at all. But there is enough to create a double ridge of thin ripples on the near side through which a "hitched" fly skims in textbook fashion. Over the years, I have hooked at least forty fish at this precise spot. Unlike the lightning quick rises from beside the Bathtub Rock, the fish of the Steady usually rise in a regal manner with the typical "curl" or full circle as they drift up with the current, gulp the fly, and turn, exposing dorsal and tail tip as they attempt to resume their station. But, like the Bathtub fish, they lie so tight to the rock that one must assume it is a security blanket. Certain fish, for their own reasons, home in on this rock as a beacon. Take one fish there and a half hour later you'll probably take another, and the next year will be more of the same. The reason the fish are there, or beside any rock for that matter, is because the speed and vagaries of the

Duncan Barnes, obviously happy with an eighteen-pound Iceland salmon. The stout little island pony doesn't appear to be overly impressed. Nice haircut!

current simply feel right to them—not unlike receiving a back rub or massage from a pair of skilled hands. Some give better back rubs than others, and so it must be with the salmon as the water flows and undulates against their bodies.

Some salmon may seek the cover or comfortable feel of the current beside or near a chunk of rock or driftwood, but I'm quite sure that overhanging protection is of little consequence to them. In rivers of any size or bottom configuration, many salmon don't seem to seek structures. They can select resting spots in the middle of a gravel patch, over a nest of football-size rocks, or even over sandy flats growing thick with undulating weeds and grass if the current feels right. They do, however, appear to avoid muddy bottoms or places where too much streamside debris has gathered. The color and texture of the bottom can also be factors where a choice is available. Quebec's north shore rivers, for example, feature stretches where rusty-hued sand is prevalent. Some pools have only small patches of this bottom material, while others have vast expanses of it. Where there is a lot of this sand, there doesn't seem to be much of a pattern; but where it's scarce, resting salmon are drawn to it like magnets to steel. Perhaps they spawn in this material (although I've never seen it happen), and then again, maybe it has a comforting feeling when they rub their fins and bellies over it. Whatever the reason, when I see a patch of rusty sand in an otherwise nondescript pool, I'll certainly cast over it with extra care. My favorite Steady pool has a strip of this rusty sand running right down the middle of it, and that's another reason I'm so fond of that piece of water.

Nothing in this world is so useful to a salmon angler on new water as a competent guide. We'll get deeper into the subject of guides at another spot in this offering, but knowing the river in question and, most important, knowing where the salmon have traditionally stopped is more than half the battle. Every salmon river has its Bathtub Rock, its Harry's Ledge, Frank's Run, or whatever. These are the precise locations bright salmon (most of them having been away from the river for at least eighteen months) return to unerringly. There's the odd fish that has made the river-to-ocean—back-to-river trip more than once, but even in this case we must ponder the attraction these places have. Ponder? We stand in awe of it! The good guides and those lucky enough to live adjacent to a salmon river know these spots as intimately as they know their own closet. I can't count the times I've been amazed by the accurate predictions of certain guides about how to cast to a particular location and even which size and pattern the fish will rise to. Predicting the pattern is usually more a matter of good luck than management, but size isn't, nor is the advice on where to cast.

Occasionally, a salmon will be in a place it shouldn't, but on the whole, don't expect to find many fish in slow-moving or what is usually referred to as "slack" water. They like to feel some current. Then again, oxygen-rich water may be more the reason they select certain sites. I think this is particularly true when fish first enter fresh water. At the "sea" pools in many salmon rivers, the salmon not only race about with

The famous bridge or "town" pool at Matane, Quebec. All of the fish entering this productive river must run the gauntlet. Most make it. Not all salmon fishing is in the wilderness.

Guy Silliker nets a salmon from the Little Southwest Miramichi for Ned Smith. Poor form here, both angler and guide are standing in the canoe. The angler fishing the pool on the right is no doubt hoping they'll both go overboard after hooking fish from "his" pool.

Snapped at the moment of strike, this photo proves that Atlantic salmon can be quite close to the shore if the lie is suitable. No more than five feet of line plus leader were needed to reach this fish.

abandon but frequently take flies with great gusto. They haven't settled in yet to a more reserved river existence and can be found in all parts of such pools.

At the Hunt River Falls in Labrador, the four-hundred-yard stretch of water immediately below the formidable precipice that forms the gateway to the upper river doesn't look like a good salmon pool to many anglers. Oh, it has some rocks, ledges, and craggy nooks, but there is a lot of shallow, bouncy water that shouldn't be "holding" water. Yet it is; and when bright fish are in the pool, they can be anywhere. In fact, the most frequent mistake made by casters here is tossing their flies into the middle of the run first. Making the first cast drift along the shore, no more than three feet from the rocky bank, is most productive. Hook the near fish first if you can, and work into the middle and far side later. This is good advice on all salmon rivers. Salmon don't spook as easily as trout, but eventually they will tire of seeing a line drift over them too many times. Good friend Tommy Goins, who "owns" Camp Pool Two on the Mecatina River, has taken two dozen fish from that pool from a hot spot that's not more than fifteen inches from the shore. So much for long casting!

3

How They Are Fished

At least seventy-five percent of the Atlantic salmon that become attached to wet flies do so with little help from the angler. This is so because most salmon anglers are fishing the wet fly across and downstream. The salmon rises to intercept the fly drifting with or being pulled against the current, and, having done so, turns to resume its previous position and is hooked. The first indication the angler has that a salmon is there is a forceful tug on the rod. The salmon has actually hooked itself. Creating that happy sequence of events is what wet-fly fishing for salmon is about.

Some anglers schooled well in trout techniques adjust quickly to salmon and some do not. If you are highly skilled at hooking Atlantic salmon, you can ignore this chapter. I really hope you don't, since you may notice where I've been going wrong for thirty years and might write to tell me about it. There are days when salmon are absolute pushovers, and then there are days when dozens of splashes, swirls, bulges, and other heartpounding fishy antics cause one to believe some other sport should be pursued.

In the typical salmon-rise scenario, our hero's fly is coasting along some forty feet distant at, or just beneath, the surface. The current is fast enough to move the fly at a

The author nets a grilse for bush pilot Charlie Coe. This fish was lying less than eighteen inches from the rock we're standing on.

steady pace with its hook pointed downward, allowing the fish to see the full profile of the pattern. As the fly reaches the end of its drift, it picks up speed and begins that familiar little "button-hook" maneuver. This sudden change of speed is what frequently stirs the fish into action. If a salmon is beneath the fly at this moment (or perhaps tracking it) and decides that further investigation is called for, up it rises with beautiful timing . . . gulp. If the angler is looking elsewhere, admiring the cloud pattern or distracted by a duck flying upriver, the fish may be hooked automatically, and he congratulates himself on a job well done. If he's keeping a sharp eye on the fly or its wake, as he should be, he may or may not hook the fish. Bashline Rule Number 1: When fishing the wet fly downstream on a reasonably straight line, do not strike or move the fly in any way at the sight of the fish or disturbance in the water. *Wait* until you feel pressure!

I'll admit there are a lot of conditions covered in that rule, but the fact is, the situation described is most common. The actions of the fish and the drag of the line will stick the point of a sharp hook into the corner of the fish's jaw, and all that's left to do is raise the rod tip smartly, engaging the barb. Note I said "raise the rod tip smartly," not jerk it with enough force to cross the salmon's eyes. Compared to many other fish, a salmon's jaw is not overly rugged. A good hook purchase will hold well enough for a reasonable time, but an overly powerful strike will be counterproductive.

The supreme bugaboo of salmon hooking for most trout-trained anglers is a too-quick reaction. Even the smallish grilse are twenty inches long instead of ten, and while they can move very fast indeed, they still require a bit more time to make their turn and engulf the fly in moving water. The typical riseform sees a portion of the back break the surface as the fish turns to strike. The dorsal fin is often visible and so is the tip of the tail. All of this is seen quickly, but in the novice angler's eyes it seems like it's happening in a flash. He reacts the customary way and snaps his rod up with a mighty stroke and feels nothing. He struck before the fly was securely in the fish's mouth and perhaps before the fly was touched at all. There's also the chance that the salmon didn't touch the fly on purpose, and ripping the fly through the water may startle the fish so badly that it won't come back again. Be patient!

There are few true axioms in salmon fishing, but one that is truer than most is that a fish that came once for a fly can probably be coaxed into coming again. In the case of grilse, I've seen some rise fifteen or more times before finally being hooked. And each time they came to the same fly presented the same way. Large fish will sometimes try again, but generally they rise less often in sequence.

Now, our hero has seen a fish rise to his fly a time or two. The adrenalin in the brain and rod hand has reached a critical level, and his reflexes are on the edge of exploding. If the fish does rise again, it's in mortal danger of having its jaw removed if the hook finds its mark. A good move on the part of the hyped angler is to check his casting for a few minutes, allow his heart to slow down a beat or two, and remember to wait until he feels the solid pull of the fish before doing anything.

Okay, you've waited. Cast precisely to the spot first hit, allow the fly to drift in *exactly* the same way, and do nothing except breathe until that pull is felt. There he is. The water bulges, six inches of fish back appears and vanishes, and the rod tip arches downward with a solid surge. Lift the tip *smoothly* and *smartly*, pulling in slack line with the other hand and . . . you've got him!

The distance between the angler and a rise can be difficult to judge. There is a tendency to pull a few more feet of line from the reel before making the next cast to the hot spot—I've found myself doing it many times. Don't. An anxious fish will still come to the overcast fly, but the best way of seeing the second rise is to stick with the same length of line and as close to the same drift as possible. When a salmon chooses its lie, it will return to within a fraction of an inch of that location. It may or may not move out of its zone to chase a fly, with the odds being in favor of it staying put. Fish fresh from the ocean in the near sea pools can do a lot of darting about, seizing flies in the most unlikely spots and chasing them for thirty feet or more, but once adjusted to the river current and the continual taste of fresh water, seldom do they move much from their lies. And here is the beauty of becoming familiar with a particular river.

Year after year, fish that cannot possibly recall specific rocks, ledges, or bottom configurations return to holding spots as surely as any swallow that ever went back to Capistrano. It is a marvelous happening for the angler to observe but, of course, a fatal habit for the salmon. We know where a fish is going to be, and armed with the knowledge, we will concentrate on these surefire locations and fish them with more diligence. If we don't know where these places are on a "new" river, it's a good bet that the guides do.

There is a pool on the Little Southwest Miramichi named Blackmoor's. It is near the village of Silliker, upstream from Red Bank, and for all of the fifties and sixties was one of the most productive pools in all of New Brunswick. When the pool was viewed across at normal flow, there was practically nothing that would distinguish it. There was a lovely deep oxbow pool below it and a long stretch of mild riffles on the upstream side. What formed the Blackmoor's Pool was a diagonal bar of small rocks and sand that stretched from one bank to the other. The gravelly bar changed its precise angle from year to year because of ice chunks churning in the spring, but as sure as the change of seasons, the bar was there each spring when the flow reached normal velocity. This is a hydraulic phenomenon that I can't account for. It happens in salmon rivers, and all rivers for that matter, in ways that astound engineering minds.

To digress for a moment, it has been well observed that human attempts to create salmon pools by bulldozing, excavating, and dam building seldom achieve the desired results. Spring floods and other natural occurrences can change the face of a river at times, but once established, many pools don't appear to change over the years. Nor do the salmon. They will take up new locations if the riverbed changes naturally, but seldom can they be coaxed into stopping off at a spot of man's choosing. They are going to lie where they jolly well please, and you and I are not going to change their minds. And so it was (and I hope still is) at Blackmoor's Pool.

The lower Oxbow Pool would hold salmon at times during July, but it was much better known as a September pool, when the water was lower. Blackmoor's was the first really good holding pool upstream from the tidal water at Red Bank. And what a pool it was. There were mornings and evenings when a full platoon of anglers could count on hooking at least a fish each, and some of the better fishermen would hook a half dozen or more. It was *ritual* fishing with all anglers wading the river above the bar and then moving across the bar, casting to the precise edge of the lip. Everyone's flies would move down and across with the current for a drift of about twenty feet each cast. Then, a step or two to the right, and five or six more casts would be made. This was public water with the locals and the visiting "sports" all doing the same dance routine. It was not the sort of fishing that would appeal to the private sort of angler— there was plenty of that to be had farther upstream. But it was a special kind of fishing fun with a lot of conversation, good-natured kidding, and, most exciting of all, action when a new pod of fish came to the bar.

As you began the trip across the bar, the first few shuffles and the accompanying casts seldom produced anything. Nor did the final shuffles as you reached the end of the bar and the near shore. It was the center of the bar where the most activity took place, so naturally when the caster got into the good water, the fly was watched more intently. Others fishing beside you, about twelve feet apart usually, could also see if a fish rose to anyone's fly. If one came and wasn't hooked by the persons on your left or right, you hoped that the fish would make a mistake on the next cast and grab your fly instead of your neighbor's. In ten years of fishing Blackmoor's, I don't think this ever happened. In spite of the large numbers of fish caught there and the huge pods of salmon that would arrive en masse on occasions, each fish would pick a spot and stay there until it was caught or decided to move upstream. If a particular fish was in a taking mood, the fly it chose had to drift or be pulled directly over its head. If a fish rose, the fly had to be returned for a second chance to precisely the same spot . . . and I don't mean even a foot away.

Another feature of Blackmoor's Pool was that it wasn't the sort of place that held salmon for long. Some anglers were convinced that because the fish were so heavily pounded there, they simply got tired of seeing all those flies and moved on. Earl Matchett, the dean of Little Southwest guides, for many years thought differently. He had fished the pool long before the Yankee sports were coming in numbers, and allowed that the fish had never tarried more than a day at the most. There were no serious rapids above or below Blackmoor's, so the fish had no great reason to spend a long time resting there, Earl reasoned. The water flowing over the bar had a good "feel" to it, he thought, but not good enough to make the fish want to stay for an extended period. All delightful supposition and, perhaps, true. It's nevertheless wonderful con-

Anglers take turns going across "the bar" on the Little Southwest Miramichi. Etiquette requires that the angler on your left becomes gillie when netting time arrives.

versation material and still more fuel for our tale-telling by the salmon camp fire . . . if we need more. Ah, the mysteries!

The tales, some true and some not, about Blackmoor's Pool could be told far into many nights by anglers who fished there. My favorite took place on what began as a dull evening. I was fishing with Bob and Andy Korosec of New Jersey and staying in their camp, which was only a half-mile walk from Blackmoor's. There had been the usual contingent of anglers working the bar that evening, but nothing was showing and the pool was dead as a stone. Nearly everyone gave up and departed except old Earl, Guy Silliker (known affectionately as the Miramichi Radio—Guy talked a lot), and me. We had fished our arms off and were sitting there on chunks of driftwood lamenting the lack of action. Perhaps an hour of daylight remained when suddenly, at the top of the Oxbow Pool, about three hundred yards downstream, several salmon free-jumped into the air with reckless fury. At least a dozen fish were in the air at once, and just as quickly as it had begun, the leaping stopped. "Let's get after 'em, boys," Earl said, and jumped up to wade out to casting position. Guy and I followed. We waded to the center of the bar and began to cast with jaws set tight. In less than three minutes, we were all hooked up with the rods literally jerking forward in unison. We each beached a fish by wading across to the near side and after a quick check of fly and leader waded back to do it again . . . and again . . . and again. I can't remember precisely how many fish we hooked, landed, and lost in one hour of frantic action, but they were several. Earl kept hollering, "Keep on fishing, hurry up, it won't last long!"

He was right. The action stopped as quickly as it began, and the pool reverted to its previous dullness. There had been a high tide that afternoon, and Earl's explanation was that this particular group of fish found the tide to their liking and moved upriver fast. They had apparently covered the three miles from tidewater to Blackmoor's in one hurried dash and arrived just in time to greet us before we called it a day. They stayed in the pool for an hour, or so it seemed, and then continued upriver. In such a situation, salmon fishing can be like deer hunting: a matter of being in the right place at the right time. The same kinds of flurries also happen on other rivers, but they were common on the Little Southwest.

While the Little Southwest is not known today as a "big fish" river, plenty of twenty- and twenty-five-pounders have been caught there over the years. The largest salmon I ever actually saw come for my fly did so on the Little Southwest. I still tremble thinking about it over twenty years later. No, I didn't capture it, but the story is worth telling because it further illustrates what not to do when a fish rises.

After a fruitless morning I was headed back to the Korosec camp for some lunch and a snooze. It was a warm July day in New Brunswick, in the upper seventies at least, and I guessed that few fish would be interested in my flies during midday. As I walked past the long, nearly still run above Blackmoor's Pool, I noticed what appeared to be a sunken log resting on the bottom. It was about thirty feet from the bank. The log hadn't been there that morning and was resting in a curious place—just a patch of reddish gravel. My mouth must have fallen open when I saw a thin line of white appear as the fish opened its mouth and the "log" suddenly became a huge salmon. It was well over a yard long, and as I stared into the shallow water, I could see the entire form clearly. A mature, hook-billed male salmon that had to weigh more than thirty-five pounds!

High noon, bright sun, and a gigantic salmon resting in less than three feet of water, nearly slack water at that. A highly vulnerable spot for a salmon of any size to pause and a place where no one had ever seen a salmon before. Of course, I'd cast to it. Good heavens, any salmon chaser worth his waders would have to try for this one. I cast. I cast some more. And still more. The fish did nothing except move its mouth at a slow, steady rate gulping water in a relaxed way. It was absolutely motionless otherwise.

I changed flies several times and tried every trick I could think of. I brought the fly across the big fish's nose at high speed. I tried it slowly. I drifted dry flies of several sizes over, beside, and behind it. None of my best salmon-coaxing strategies as much as caused a glance. Remembering my own advice to salmon beginners, I also tried different casting positions. I moved farther upstream in order to try a longer drift and a different angle of approach. Several moves in this direction were equally ignored. I rested the fish for ten-minute intervals and tried everything once more. Frustration.

It occurred to me that if I were to wade across the river below the fish and cast from the other side, a new "look" at the fly would be possible. It was easy to wade here since the water was barely at my thighs, and as I did so, I had an even better look at the fish. It seemed to be growing before my eyes, and I was mentally seeing the scales approach the forty-pound mark. It was by far the largest Atlantic salmon I had ever seen in the water!

The same fly I had started with, a very ordinary Blue Charm hairwing on a number 6 hook, was reattached. After selecting my casting position at about twenty-five feet across and slightly upstream from the big salmon's resting spot, I made a quick check of the leader and tugged on the knots. Everything seemed to be in good order, and the first cast from this location was delivered. As the fly drifted slowly over it, the salmon waggled his fins a bit and moved forward a few inches. My heart and Adam's apple changed places. The next cast was as close to being a duplicate of the first as I could manage, and this time the fish actually rose up three or four inches for another look, his dorsal fin breaking the surface. I was near choking on surplus adrenalin. Somehow, I made a third cast that was reasonably close to the first two. I *knew* the fish was going to take. As the fly reached the imaginary window of opportunity, the great fish rose in a slow, dignified manner and opened its mouth to engulf the Blue Charm. I actually saw the fly suspended in what appeared to be a ten-inch gap between upper and lower jaws, and I proceeded to do exactly the wrong thing. I nervously jerked the rod in anticipation of the strike and snatched that fly right out of its mouth! That was it.

The grilse netted here was hooked at the very lip of Camp Pool Two on the Mecatina River and instead of running upstream, dashed into the fast water below. It was finally "led" back up by applying even pressure.

With a purposeful wag of a tail roughly the size of a snow shovel, the salmon moved upstream and out of sight. Forever.

All I'd had to do was nothing. If I had just waited until that huge maw had clamped on the fly, he'd have been mine. At least he would have been hooked, and the open water there would have provided an excellent setting for the battle. But it was not to be. I still have dreams about that fly hanging there, about to be gulped. Having a clear view of a big fish about to seize one's fly is a thoracic thrill of considerable magnitude. Two decades later, the experience is still recalled with a combination of delight and regret. It points out once more that to strike too soon at a salmon's rise is far worse than to strike too late!

To strike at all is a popular topic wherever salmoneers gather. Indeed, some pools feature currents that create a totally self-hooking situation. The conditions that exist in such spots are such that the fish turning its weight on the fly and water pressure against the line do the job automatically. In such places the angler is well advised to fish by feel rather than sight. A perfect example of why it's more fun to be lucky than skillful also comes from the Little Southwest and it involves my great, late friend Ned Smith.

Ned was, and still is, for my money, the best wildlife portrait artist ever to make Pennsylvania his home. Specifically, no artist before or since has ever painted ruffed grouse with such a depth of understanding. Ned was also a highly accomplished naturalist and an excellent angler. I was delighted when he agreed to join me for his first fling at Atlantic salmon. I knew he'd take to the sport with gusto, and it's always fun to be there when such a marriage is consummated.

We arrived at the camp about five-thirty in the afternoon. A note tacked to the door advised us that our friends were upriver and would return at dark. I had fished the Southwest many times before, so this was no problem. We'd simply rig up and fish Blackmoor's that evening by ourselves. I knew the water reasonably well and was confident we'd have a decent shot at a fish. But my hopes were dampened when we saw the condition of the river. It was exceptionally low and Blackmoor's Pool was a shadow of its usual self. The diagonal bar was totally exposed, and the water below it was close to dead calm. Too calm for any fish to stop there.

Downstream was the Oxbow Pool, and although it was low as well, there was still a flow of some consequence in the center of the deep water. I remarked to Ned that while this was considered by local anglers to be a September pool (better in the fall than the summer), fish were taken there occasionally at other times. Having never fished for salmon anywhere, Ned was not close-minded about traditions. He simply waded into the pool and began casting a Black Bear (Red-Butt) I'd handed him. Ned was a fine fly caster, and as trout fishermen always do, he began casting at the tail of the pool instead of at the top of the current. I quickly pointed out his "error," but as I was doing so, there was a huge boil about a foot behind his drifting fly. I didn't finish the fifty-cent lecture on where to cast but hollered at him to make the next cast just like he'd made the last one. Wonder of wonders. A beginner at the salmon chase had a fish interested in his fly after making fewer than a half dozen casts in low water, and in a pool not noted for holding fish in July. And to top it off, the rise had the earmarks of being made by a sizable fish!

To Ned's great credit, he plunked that fly exactly back to the right spot, and the salmon rose within a magnificent boil, hooking itself solidly. Ned had done quite a bit of saltwater fishing in recent years, and he was skilled at handling large fish by fighting them from the reel. The first run was a classic, punctuated by a series of wild leaps. The big grin on Ned's face was a sure indication another salmon angler had been born. After another series of shorter runs and three more leaps, a sleek fourteen-pounder was skidded onto the sand. The grin was still there, and I had one too. The first pool was fished, the first fish hooked and landed, all within an hour after arriving in New Brunswick.

His ears still hurting a bit from the long dissertations on salmon-fishing techniques I had presented during the 850-mile car ride from Pennsylvania, Ned couldn't resist the chance to get even. "Gee, I was under the impression that this Atlantic salmon fishing was difficult. Why, there's nothing to it!"

Having fished for many different species across the country, Ned knew better, and we both sat on the bank for more than twenty minutes admiring the fish and soaking up the joy of the moment. Later that evening we got a second helping of euphoria when the rest of the camp regulars returned from their upriver trip. Four of them had managed to hook and lose one small grilse each, but no one had even seen a fish approaching the fourteen-pound mark in four days. When I pulled Ned's fish out of the ice chest, they nearly fainted and almost did so again when I told them that Ned had caught the fish in the Oxbow Pool. There hadn't been a fish caught there since the previous fall. As with dice, horseracing, or other activities where Lady Luck plays a role, the salmon angler gets lucky once in a while too. The area between skill and luck is murky indeed.

The placement of the cast can always be attributed to luck on the part of an inexperienced salmon angler, but after we've spent some time at the sport, we come to know how important this is. An adult salmon will seldom move far from its chosen lie to inspect a fly. Grilse sometimes will and especially will very bright fish not far from salt water, but even these more exuberant fish can be extremely fussy about where that fly is cast. Once during a period of high water on the Mecatina, Sylvia was fishing the lower end of the Steady Pool from a small boat. Curry, her guide, had anchored beside a strip of reddish gravel where a pod of ten or so grilse could be seen fanning in the current. The fish didn't move toward any of her flies until she cast a full twenty feet upstream above their position and jerked the fly back over them with a quick retrieve.

She reported that she was able to get exactly the right movement and the right depth on about one cast out of ten. The fish would not take the fly on the surface nor did they want it deep. It had to scoot into the school of fish at a level barely above their noses and arrive at that depth from a nearly perfect ninety-degree angle. When all of this was done right, a grilse would break out of the pack and grab the fly with total confidence. She hooked four fish by repeating the correct moves, and after she handed the rod over to Curry, he hooked three more by duplicating her technique. It's worth repeating, that if a fish rises or flashes at your fly, note the spot with great care and cast to it again, doing exactly what you did the first time. If a slight pull was made on the leader to move the fly a couple inches, do it again. If you threw a little slack into the leader at mid-drift, do it again. Do everything just the same for a dozen casts before you try some new routine. Each salmon at each location is a law unto itself and will rise or not rise as it chooses. The technique that will bring one fish to your fly may or may not work on another fish in the same pool or even at the same lie. It is these traits that put the Atlantic salmon into a behavioral category shared with few other fish.

Some other anadromous species, such as the western steelhead and the American shad, display a few of the Atlantic salmon's peculiarities, but no other fish has them all. In the salt water, the tarpon, bonefish, and certainly the permit share some of the moody idiosyncrasies of the Atlantic salmon, but the striking difference is that the salmon does not feed upon entering fresh water until after its spawning chores are over. Until then it is incapable of feeding because of a physical constriction of its esophagus. The other fish mentioned, with the exception of the American shad, can and do take nourishment at all times. This is the most baffling question and the one salmon anglers have been asking themselves and each other since the sport began: If the salmon is not feeding in fresh water, why on earth do they take anything into their mouths and particularly our flies?

Primitive people probably saw Atlantic salmon rise to the surface to seize a floating twig, leaf, or feather and wondered about it. We can only guess when the wonder gave rise to experimentation in a way that suggested modern salmon fly fishing. But someone did experiment, and thank goodness for it, or we'd still be using spears.

We haven't advanced far beyond early anglers' speculations about *why* these fish take a fly. We haven't and it's most likely we won't, because the salmon aren't talking, and reading their thoughts is an impossibility. With the full understanding that this area of discussion is full of actual and symbolic pitfalls, I submit that all fish, and particularly salmon, don't act, *they react*. In that sentence, I fervently believe, lies the answer to this long-standing question. Fish rise to a particular fly at a particular moment because the reaction button is pushed. There is no thought process involved here. It is not in any way like a fox coming to a baited trap, or one of us sitting down to a plate of bacon and eggs in the morning because we're hungry. The salmon has no predetermined desire to eat a Jock Scott or a Rusty Rat number 6. It simply sees a form, which triggers a reaction mechanism . . . and it reacts. It is this reaction that separates salmon from their close cousins the trout. Trout take an artificial fly because they think it is some form of insect. They seize a streamer fly because they suppose it to be a minnow. The form suggests food. If any of the traditional salmon patterns suggest fish food of any sort found on this planet, I've never been fortunate enough to see it!

We'll dip much deeper into the subject of flies in another chapter, but to continue with the fishing of them, let's go back to the "how" part of it. We've discussed the standard wet-fly approach, so let's consider variations on that theme. The first and foremost departure from simply allowing the wet fly to drift comparatively drag-free with the current is the addition of the Riffle Hitch or, as it is known in many parts of Canada, the Portland Hitch. To my knowledge, Lee Wulff first brought this revolutionary discovery to the fishing public in an article in *Outdoor Life* back in August 1952. He and several dozen other angling writers have written of it many times since, so the hitch isn't a recent phenomenon. But it is the best trick I know to interest a salmon that has "showed" for a fly tied to a leader in a standard way and elected not to gulp it. Conversely, it is also the best stunt to try when a visible fish won't turn its head toward anything else cast its way.

The making of a Portland Hitch is simple enough. Wrap a pair of half hitches behind the head of the fly in such a way that forces the standard wet fly to plane across the surface not unlike a miniature surfboard. European salmon buffs recoil in horror at the idea of forcing a fly to create a wake, but the truth is, such a wake will catch salmon at times when nothing else will. I have spent entire weeks fishing every cast with the Portland Hitch and had no regrets about doing it. In addition, the hitch has frequently been the only link between me and total wipeout. The overseas aversion to the hitch has long been a mystery to me, since I've seen salmon in Iceland take a hitched fly with total abandon. Curt Hill, a favorite salmon-fishing companion of good standing, reported that he rose three fish and landed two on Scotland's Sneezort River after being told in terse language that "their" salmon wouldn't fall for such nonsense. While it's true that salmon in certain rivers will respond with some regularity to the trusted local methods and fly patterns, it's always worth a try to show them something different. (Hill's two salmon were, by the way, the only fish taken from that river during a two-week period.)

There are some rivers in Newfoundland and Labrador where any angler not fishing the hitch would be in a minority. As much as I like to use it, there are times when it will not work and fish that will not respond to its charms. Ideally, there must be enough current to cause the hitched fly to make its wake across the surface. Where the velocity of the current is not enough to make this happen, smooth stripping of the line is necessary in order to achieve the proper effect. How this is done is of the utmost importance with fussy fish.

I suppose the stripping speed for a hitched fly could be stated, with help from a variety of scientific instruments, in strips-per-second or in miles-per-hour. But quite honestly, I've never been good at estimating water velocity. I can see if the water is moving fast, slow, or somewhere in between, but expressing this in terms of MPH eludes me. The hitched fly can be seen, however, and how it performs can be monitored and regulated by the way the off hand strips line. The ideal speed is the one that brings the fly through the productive water at a rate just fast enough to create a visible "V" behind it. Where the water is faster, we must strip-strip-strip quite rapidly to make a good V happen. As the water slows down, a less pronounced stripping will give us a suitable V. A good rule of thumb for the first dozen tries through a pool is, *move the fly fast in fast water* and *slowly in slow water.* Avoid becoming a slave to any one style, since a slow strip in fast water and vice versa will frequently make a difference. Where salmon are the fish sought, any rule of thumb proven today will be disproven tomorrow. Murphy and I agree on this one.

I cannot count the times I've cast over a visible fish or a proven hot spot with a hitched fly and hooked or risen one when a hundred previous casts with a conventional drift were ignored. A near equal number of fish have been hooked by first raising a fish on the hitch and then switching to a non-hitched fly for the actual hooking. It's a different "look" at the same fly that made the fish pay attention. Note: I said the *same* fly. It's often merely a matter of retying the knot to bring a strike.

Guide Eldon Bobbitt, who also happens to be a master at coaxing recalcitrant salmon into making fatal mistakes, once demonstrated how critical this "different look" can be. In the upper end of Camp Pool One on the Mecatina, a salmon was giving me fits of frustration for nearly a half hour. I must have shown it ten different patterns, and every time I'd change flies, the fish would come once and sometimes twice for a very close look. I mean, *very* close. It would boil up with what appeared to be a positive strike and swap ends at the last second, literally knocking my fly into the air with its tail. I changed casting positions a dozen times, tried stripping fast and then slow. In short, I tried every trick I could think of, and still he continued to rise and look but would not grab the fly. The fishing had been slow that morning with few fish showing any interest whatsoever, so I stuck with this fickle fellow a long time. Eldon was busy with some minor boat maintenance chores while this was going on, but finally he came to my side just to listen to my mutterings. After seeing the fish come three times without getting hooked, he too agreed that this fish was certainly in a "mood to be caught," and he couldn't understand why it refused to grab the fly. I finally handed the rod to him and said, "Here, you try it, and if you hook him, I'll give you the rod!"

The rod being used that day was a ten-and-a-half footer for a 9 weight line that I'd just received from the Fenwick Company. A bit longer than I usually fish with, but it threw ninety feet of line with no effort, and a line could be mended perfectly because of the extra length. I had been casting down and over the fish from a distance of about fifty feet. A short cast for such a rod. Eldon thought about this a few seconds and

Hooked at the Bathtub Pool on the Eagle River, this fish is far from being in the net. The surrounding boulders make the battle difficult but add to the challenge. We hope Jack Eschenmann remembers where his net is.

moved to a position not twenty feet from the fish, but slightly downstream. With the long rod he flipped no more than five feet of line and the twelve-foot leader to the far side of the fish and dragged the hitched fly directly across the salmon's nose. May the fishing gods drown me if I'm not telling the truth—that damn fish took it the first cast!

Eldon didn't stop smiling for an hour after proclaiming that "that fish was a left-hander for sure and wanted to be caught by a left-handed fisherman." I have no doubt he was absolutely right. Eldon is left-handed, and what he did was drag that fly over the fish in an *opposite* direction. The fish curled to the left in taking the fly and simply would not take my flies, which were traveling to its right. Believe it or not, some salmon (and many trout) show a decided preference in which way they turn when seizing a fly. When a fish continues to rise and can't be hooked, keep on showing that fly until you discover *where* the fly looks best. (Sometimes nit-picking pays off.)

4

The Rod for Atlantic Salmon

What constitutes an ideal salmon rod or reel for Atlantic salmon fishing is a question that gets into the realm of the chicken and the egg. As with so many things involved in this game of fishing for *Salmo salar*, final answers are hard to come by. Lee Wulff proved many years ago that a handheld reel was all the tackle needed if one applied a sensitive hand. Skillful handliners, preceding Lee, were jerking salmon from rivers with regularity long before sporting tackle made an appearance on North American shores. While considerable distance can be achieved by hand tossing a fly line with fly attached, a suitable rod will deliver the fly in a much more efficient way and throw it much farther when distance is called for. We need rods, if for no other reason than having them to talk about. With the exception of flies, no other piece of gear is so mystical or non-scientific. Your perfect rod will probably not be my perfect rod, nor will the rod for one particular river or form of fly fishing be suitable for all waters. And so it goes.

The only rods to be discussed here are fly rods. If you have come this far into this book and have not yet hefted a fly rod, you're in a peck of trouble. On the western shore of the Atlantic, in the U.S. and Canada, fly fishing is the *only* legal method for taking Atlantic salmon from freshwater streams. In my heart, I earnestly believe that it should be the only method for taking them anywhere . . . period. The farming of pen-reared salmon for the marketplace will eventually produce all of our bought fish. My remarks will not be greeted with cheers in some circles, but the commercial salmon netters will be phased out of existence by the year 2020. If you'll excuse the pun, that's my vision of the future. However, let's forget the politics and economics of Atlantics for the moment and get back to tackle. The rod first.

For ninety-five percent of the Atlantic salmon fishing in the world, a nine-foot rod casting a 9 weight line will do quite nicely. It's entirely possible to cover the world of salmon fishing with your favorite trout rod or with one of the ponderous, two-handed salmon killers of European persuasion. Considering these extremes would give us coverage from four-foot flea rods to heroic shafts ranging from twelve to twenty-two feet. There are places where rods of both sorts would be useful and even desirable, but on most waters too much or too little rod would be an annoyance and a handicap. As a stunt, I've caught salmon on rods measuring less than five feet. I've also spent a small amount of time slinging fly lines on prodigious poles of fourteen feet or more. Using the big rods is also something of a stunt as far as I'm concerned, since it is almost impossible to lay a fly down with finesse. These rods will fight a big fish to the beach in short order, but casting them and simply holding them for a full day requires the strength of a decathlon champion. Fishing is supposed to be fun.

That bit of dogma out of the way, let's look more closely at that nine-foot ideal. Over nearly half a century of wiggling fly rods, owning dozens, and trying out several hundred more for friends and magazine articles, I've come to a few personal conclusions. I do not like:

1. Keeper rings next to the grip that stick out straight. (They can foul the line and always do when a big fish is hooked.)
2. Reel seats that come loose.
3. Tiny guides that foul leader knots and line loops.
4. Overly thick grips, which eventually tire the hand.
5. Short grips that don't provide a shift of hand position.
6. Exceptionally stiff rods that don't flex on short casts.

I would be hard pressed to place these rod shortcomings in order of importance, because all of them have caused great grief. Stiff keeper rings or wire loops are an absolute abomination. I am not a perfect caster and for some unknown reason always seem to have stray loops of line hanging about in strange places. When I try to "shoot" line a few extra feet and have the slack fly through the guides in an artful way, those stiff wire hookkeepers invariably foul the moving line and screw up the works. Before I use any rod so equipped, I carefully take a pair of pliers, squeeze the wire together, and jerk it out. A rod keeper of any kind is really unnecessary on a rod used for salmon fishing, since the hook should be hung on the fifth guide and the leader passed behind the reel seat for easy carrying and storage while in camp. Some of the better rods have the floppy ring that has been the traditional hookkeeper for a century or more . . . and these cause no particular trouble. Nevertheless I seldom use them.

Loose reel seats shouldn't be a problem in these days of super glues and epoxies, but for some reason, certain rod manufacturers attach reel seats with inferior stickum. Regluing a loose reel seat is an easy matter but annoying if it's necessary during fishing. Murphy's laws include one about loose reel seats that states: "If a reel seat comes loose or falls off (with reel attached), it will always happen when the largest fish of your life has been hooked." Locking reel seats are best on salmon rods. If one does not lock, a few wraps of electrical tape around both sides of the reel foot will keep it on for a week. In fact, wrapping the tape over any reel seat is good insurance.

Any rod used for salmon or saltwater species should have guides ample in quantity and size. With too few guides, the line flops about during casting and causes the rod to bend unnaturally. If the guides are too small, smooth casting and fish fighting can be difficult.

There is no reason to use a bulky knot where leader attaches to line, but even the most carefully made nail knot or epoxy splice can go "bump" when a fish is close to netting or tailing time. At the end of a prolonged battle, hooks have a way of coming loose, and that slight vibration as the line knot slips over the tip-top can undo things. Most quality rods built for larger fish are customarily supplied with quality guides of plated metal or stainless steel (the best), with the stripping guide, the one closest to the grip, lined with ceramic material or aluminum oxide. On older rods genuine agate will be seen, and they were, and are, great. If you're still using a rod with an agate stripping guide, God bless you, but watch out for cracks there. It can strip the finish from a fly line in short order.

While it might seem that the diameter of a fly rod grip should be calibrated to the size of one's hand, this isn't the case. I have a hand about the size of a catcher's mitt, but a too-thick grip is extremely tiring for me. In the typical thumb-on-top grip, I like to have the fingers just touching the heel of the palm when casting. If the grip is too thick to allow this, the full casting potential of the rod can't be realized. If you cast with the index finger on the top of the rod, the pinkie finger and one next to it should lightly touch the palm. If this doesn't happen with your favorite rod, a bit of careful sanding is called for. Don't ever be afraid to modify a rod grip to suit your hand or casting style. After all, you're the one who must fish with it, so hang what others might say about your alterations.

I'm not fussy about the overall shape of a fly rod grip as long as it isn't too thick near the reel seat. When casting a nine-foot rod and 9 weight line beyond fifty feet, I grasp the rod in such a way that the heel of the palm is pressing hard against the reel seat and part of the reel itself. By holding the rod as far back as I can, I'm convinced I get the maximum power out of the rod and the fullest flex possible. Of course, this won't suit those who cast with index finger on top of the grip. I switch to this grip for very short casts where a higher degree of accuracy is called for; therefore I like grips that taper to the diameter of the rod's butt section. To their credit, Orvis equips many of their rods with such a grip, and it works fine for both methods. Here again, some rasp and sandpaper work can do wonders.

I have some concerns about discussing the nebulous area of rod action. No other topic of tackle conversation (save the flies) becomes so opinionated. The problem is, rod action can be explained partly in scientific and mechanical terms, but then a point is reached where personalities and angling subtleties take over. As a comparison, some shooters can score well with any shotgun. Others must have "old reliable" in order to break 25 straight at trap or skeet. Shooting a shotgun at moving targets is an art form and not subject to mathematical formulas. Human eyes, muscle structures, reflex times, and physical sizes vary infinitely, making general advice on how to shoot well just that. The same factors apply to casting a fly rod, presenting a fly in an attractive manner, and hooking fish with it. Your ideal rod may not be mine and vice versa. In addition, the rod that suits one for trout fishing, bass bugging, drifting flies deep for steelheads, or taming a brawling tarpon may not fill the bill for salmon fishing at all. And since this book is about Atlantic salmon fishing, I'll try to confine my ramblings to that. Since also this is my book, the remarks will be highly personal.

A too-stiff rod is not a good salmon rod. Neither is one that has no backbone or that flops about haphazardly when wiggled in the store or when line is flowing through the guides. Wiggling a rod in the store, by the way, proves little unless the one doing the shaking has shaken a heap of rods. Flexing it back and forth tells us nothing. Snapping the tip forward smartly in a simulation of casting can show us something about the rod's recovery time, but even that's difficult to determine without actually casting it. Having a reel in place can change the feel of a rod totally, and putting a line on it changes the picture still again. Ideally, a rod costing more than the price of a case of good wine should be tested before the money for it is laid down. (The wine should be tested too, incidentally.)

At the risk of sounding like a broken record on this business of stiffness, I must point out that when the graphite rod era began, not quite twenty years ago at this printing, most manufacturers didn't seem to care much about finesse. Like pioneers in all fields, they were much more concerned with blockbuster effects, and they built a rugged shaft that would throw a fly line into the middle of next week. This is an impartial broadside that applies to all those manufacturers. The old rod makers and the new kids on the block did the same thing. They cranked out slick-looking black sticks and hired an accomplished caster to tour the sport shows and wow the pants off everyone with hundred-foot casts. This was heady stuff and, frankly, sold a lot of rods to awestruck anglers. There were a number of things wrong with these early graphite rods, the most glaring of these being: flies came crashing down with a vengeance and the rigid sticks required near perfect timing (and a staccato casting style) that many fishermen couldn't duplicate. Hooking fish on downstream casts, which is the way ninety percent of salmon are hooked, was difficult. Within three years, the makers of quality rods realized the shortcomings of early graphites, and some outstanding rods for trout and salmon fishing began to appear. Happily, most makers have softened their fly rods a tad since those days, but the final test must still be a session of actual casting with the line you intend to fish with.

Understanding my description of the action that suits me—and some of you, I hope—requires some knowledge of music. If you don't know waltz time, ask someone who does to count it out for you. Rig the rod with reel, line, and a ten- or twelve-foot leader. Strip out forty feet of line. To the end of the leader attach an air-resistant dry fly, with the hook point nipped off or covered by a small gob of wool yarn. Begin false casting in your usual manner. If the rod moves the line back and forth smoothly, in reasonably tight loops, extending fully forward and backward in an even one-two-three, one-two-three cadence, it'll suit me just fine. If the line tugs at the forward stroke before you reach a full one-two-three count or does the same on the back cast, then the rod is probably a bit on the stiff side. If the count must be slowed down, it may be a shade too soft to add any distance when line must be "shot" through the guides.

I can hear the long distance casting experts clucking their tongues over this and saying, "I can make any rod cast to waltz time by simply increasing or slowing my wrist and arm movement to compensate for the rod's action." Certainly you can, and so can any good caster, but the operative words are *in your usual manner.* Any caster who has handled a fly rod more than a couple of years has a rhythm that becomes his or hers alone, and that's what we're trying to discover: which rod works more comfortably at one's individual casting speed. But there is far more to hooking a salmon on a fly than merely casting to it, which the following describes in part. It also constitutes another reason why I submit that a castable rod that has a moderately soft action will also hook more fish for most fishermen than will a stiff one.

The rise of an Atlantic salmon to a fly drifting with the current or hanging in it is almost always a predictable maneuver. When the fish will strike is anybody's guess, but *how* it will rise is one of the few near constants in the Atlantic salmon fishing game. The fish begins to move up from its lie by cocking the pectoral and ventral fins in a planing attitude that will cause its mouth to intercept the arriving fly at a point directly above it. I've watched this perfect interception many times from tree stands and observation platforms built beside salmon pools, and I never tire of seeing it. It is a marvel of precise timing. The fly is there, the mouth opens and closes. As the salmon clamps down on the fly, it arches its body in a near perfect circle and turns in a downward spiral to resume its former position. Even a grilse of four pounds has enough bulk to make it nearly impossible to avoid showing a portion of its back when performing this pirouette. The dorsal fin frequently appears, and so might the tail. If the angler strikes when head, back, or dorsal is visible, it's a good bet that the fly isn't securely in the mouth . . . yet. The correct time to strike is when the tail vanishes and the fish has nearly completed its curling rise. In fact, a pronounced strike is seldom needed if the current is reasonably brisk. The weight of the fish and the current pressing on it will more often set the hook automatically. The chance of this happening, with a hard strike or none at all, is more likely with a soft action rod. That's because there is enough "give" or flex in the tip to bend toward the pull of the fish and the current. The softer rod will not take the fly away from the salmon too quickly and acts as a brake on the angler's reaction . . . which in the heat of the moment might not be as restrained as it could be.

Nothing is better than having the correct rod with the correct line for fly fishing, but getting them is sometimes a problem. There are ways around it, however, and sometimes what seems like a makeshift solution is the perfect one. One way to temper the quick action of a too-stiff rod is to move up a number or two in line weight. I've seen some graphite and boron rods (and a few glass sticks) transformed from a near useless salmon rod to one of acceptable action by being lined with something heavier. A rugged 7 weight rod can be slowed with an 8 weight and sometimes even a 9. But there is a problem in overlining. For short to medium casting ranges, meaning twenty to forty feet, such an outfit will usually do nicely, but beyond these, if the rod doesn't have enough backbone to carry the additional load of line, the tip begins to collapse and tossing the fly to a more distant spot becomes a problem. Heavier guides can be added, which also helps, but the very best solution is to buy the right rod in the first place.

The first "right" rod for Atlantic salmon I ever owned was a model designated the 107 by Fenwick. It was a two-piece glass rod that was nine feet long and called for a 9 weight line. And wonder of wonders to me at the time, it did indeed throw a 9 weight line better than any rod I'd cast before. This was about twenty years ago. I must have tried a dozen more rods in the interim, until Scientific Anglers came out with their "System" series of glass rods. Their 8 weight model, which was eight feet eight inches, cast so well that I began switching back and forth between the Fenwick and the SA rod on all of my salmon trips. At about the same time, I acquired a Hardy nine-footer for a 9 line that was so pretty I couldn't resist fishing with it from time to time. But alas, after using glass rods for a few years, the bamboo sticks seemed so heavy, I wondered why I was subjecting myself to such labor. But that beautiful Hardy, with its green and black windings was, and still is, a magnificent caster and will throw eighty feet of line with little effort. It also hooks fish on the downstream drift like it had a soul of its own. But it's easy to wax eloquent over bamboo rods. The skill involved in making a good one and the special pride in using them tend to carry us away at times. Loving split cane rods as much as I always have makes it difficult to admit that graphite rods have become the standard for Atlantic salmon fishing today. Fishing for salmon requires a lot of casting and rod handling. A four-ounce graphite stick is simply less fatiguing to fish with than is seven or eight ounces of bamboo, or even five or six ounces of glass.

I'm sure others have made similar statements about other products in times past, but I can't honestly see how today's graphite technology can be much improved. These thin shafts are mere feathers in the hand and when properly lined and handled will throw a fly line as far as one could ever wish. How far is that? Well, few anglers can actually cast a measured hundred feet, but most graphite rods are capable of it and more. For practical salmon angling, hooking a fish at that distance becomes chancy at best. If an angler can manage a decent seventy-five-foot cast (and all planets are in the right orbit), he'll be able to reach ninety percent of the fish in all but the largest rivers of the world.

As far as specific rods are concerned, I admit to partiality toward the graphites made by Fenwick in the 8, 9, and 10 weight range. Like the rest of the rod companies, their early graphites were a tad stiff, but with the fine guidance of Jimmy Green, one of the best fly casters I've ever watched, the company has since created some good ones. Their reel seats are sturdy and the Ferulite connection between sections has proven to be a durable joint. For a time they made a series of rods named the Traditionals. If you can find one in the nine-foot, 8 weight persuasion tucked away in a tackle store, or see one listed on a pre-owned list, grab it at any price. I wouldn't part with mine for anything; it throws an 8 line all by itself. The old Traditionals were a bit slower than the current line of Fenwick graphites, but both types will prove satisfactory.

Thomas and Thomas, the makers of today's most outstanding bamboo rods, also market graphite rods and in a variety wide enough to satisfy the most picky fly-fishing buff. The names change from time to time with all makers, but T & T usually list a half dozen rods from eight-and-a-half to nine-and-a-half-feet that range in action from soft to stiff-as-a-board. (Let me re-emphasize that there is nothing in this world wrong with fishing with any sort of action if you cast it well and it suits your style of fishing. I'm simply a stick-in-the-mud when it comes to liking the older and more "bamboo-y" feel. It's like the story about kissing the cow . . . if it feels good, fine.) These people at T & T know how to put a rod together, and their reel seats, guides, grips, and attention to details prove it.

The graphite rods built by the time-honored Orvis folks are fine salmon rods if you handle enough of them to discover which one suits best. The so-called "Orvis action" is decidedly different from that of Fenwick, T & T, and most other makers. Orvis achieves the softer feel by making blanks in such a way that the middle of the rod bends more than the tip section. The curve of an Orvis rod when fully flexed scribes a nearly perfect arc, whereas most other makers build a thinner tip that allows the rod to begin to bend at a point closer to the small end of the rod. Frankly, either action will cast a fly well in experienced hands, but the intermediate angler will notice a difference. On the bottom of the experience scale, the novice level, it won't matter either. This may sound strange, but in practice it proves to be right. Expert casters can compensate for most tackle shortcomings. They don't have to think about what they're doing. They simply adjust in mid-cast to the rod's peculiarities and make a good cast. The duffer doesn't know what to do at the outset with any rod, and until he understands the rudiments of casting, any reasonably well-made rod will be suitable. It's the person in the mid-dle—the one who knows just enough about fly casting to understand when his back-cast feels right and the rest of his technique is working well that day—who will appreciate the typical Orvis action.

Not all Orvis rods are built this way, but enough are to make the choice a broad one. If you're ordering a rod by mail and not sure which model features this slower action, make note of what you're looking for and the company will suggest the appropriate model. All reputable mail-order companies will offer this service and will also ship a replacement if the rod doesn't suit.

During the past few years we've seen a resurgence of multipiece or pack rods that are suitable for Atlantic salmon. For many years the idea of a fly rod that breaks down to four or more pieces for easy transportation has held great appeal. For the most part such rods were not worth a hoot. They were either so stiff they could be used as pool cues or so limp they wouldn't cast a fly across a pool table. I must have tried a couple dozen of them wearing many respected brand names, and I seldom found one that was marginally useful. Then, along came a parttime rod maker and saxophone player named Dave Sylvester. A peripatetic tinkerer, Sylvester cut, honed, and otherwise reworked graphite material made by the Fisher Company until he had a four-piece rod that cast like a jewel. His first Deerfield rods were strictly trout models, but in time he created a nine-and-a-half-foot four-piecer for the 9 weight line. Sylvester sent one of these to my address after reading something I'd written complaining about the lack of good pack rods. The first casting session with this rod was a revelation. After about ten minutes of tossing line on the lawn, I forgot it was a four-piecer. This Deerfield rod has since accompanied me on dozens of salmon adventures and is now nearing six years of age. Without exception, it is the smoothest casting 9 weight rod I've ever used, regardless of number of pieces.

Orvis, Thomas & Thomas, Sage, and others also market multipiece rods and, I must say, the models currently offered are quantum leaps forward from earlier efforts. I think Sylvester's lead was followed to a degree, but no matter, the angler has gained by having so many more fine choices. The interest in multipiece rods ought to be greater than it is, in my opinion, because so many anglers are climbing on airplanes to seek exotic vistas these days. Smaller cars with smaller luggage compartments are also the norm. A rod case measuring less than thirty inches is much more convenient to lug around than is a tube of four-and-a-half feet or more. You'll have an altercation with airline personnel if you try to carry a long tube onto a jet. I've never been questioned about a pack rod case that fits easily under the seat or into the overhead compartment. It's nice to know that your rod will arrive when you do. The apex of anxiety is to watch your long rod case (or worse, several of them) disappear into the maw of that ominous opening behind the ticket counter when you know full well the chances are eight to five against its getting to your destination that day.

In trying to bring my thoughts about rods to a close, I just interrupted the typing to check the rod closet. Examination revealed that I now possess fly rods made by Fenwick, Orvis, Deerfield, Hardy, Shakespeare, Thomas & Thomas, Leonard (out of business now), St. Croix, Skyline, Loomis, and probably a dozen less well known manufacturers. All of these companies make or have made fly rods that I consider to be suitable salmon tools. I don't keep a rod for long if it doesn't perform. (Save the ones that have collector value.) I swap 'em to friends and others whose casting styles are geared to the rod in question. They're happy and I'm happy.

Just to muddy the waters a bit more, I must insert that there are situations where I abandon my intense love for a soft rod and take up a stick that has a bit more spunk in the tip. This is when I expect to be casting drys more than wets. The false casting needed to dry the fly, satisfy the casting urge, and drive an air-resistant bunch of feathers into the wind requires somewhat more push. The solution is to carry an extra rod on the river. No problem. It's nice to have a spare rod along, just in case. Not that we need an excuse to buy another rod, you understand. Which reminds me, I saw this Winston rod the other day (or was it a Sage?) that seemed to have that sort of "in-between" action that just might bridge the gap and be the ideal rod for wets *and* drys, if one carried an extra reel loaded with a 10 weight line. Then I could . . . and on into the night!

5

Reels

The fly reel, unlike the fly rod, is an easily categorized piece of equipment. It is basically a winch, a mechanical device that has been in use as long as the wheel and perhaps longer. Since fishermen are an enterprising lot, it should not come as a great surprise to discover that a way of cranking fish to a boat or the shore with handmade line and simple winch was common before the wheelbarrow or rudimentary cart. Because so much of our fly-fishing gear and lore had its beginnings in England, it's logical to assume that salmon equipment also gestated there. It did, and without dipping deeply into musty history pages, let it be noted that the British "Nottingham" reel, a remarkably simple device fashioned out of wood, served as a basic salmon reel for nearly two centuries. It didn't rust or corrode, so some exist today in excellent condition. Most successful fly reels are merely refinements of the Nottingham, made now from metal or synthetic materials instead of wood.

There are really only four attributes a reel must have in order to function well as a salmon-fishing tool:

1. It must have enough spool capacity to hold at least one hundred yards of backing and a full fly line.

2. It must have some sort of adjustable braking or "drag" feature.
3. It must be made from a material that won't fracture when dropped on rocks or boat bottom.
4. It must be made with enough precision to allow the reel spool to rotate rapidly within the frame without binding.

Personally, I add three additional features: The reel must have handle(s) long enough to grasp easily but not so long as to protrude and snag the line at inopportune moments. It must have a click device. (I am adamant about the click. Without the *zzzzzz* of a running reel when a fish makes his first dash for freedom, salmon fishing would be fifty percent less exciting. The sound of the reel is the song of the salmon.) Last, the reel must be convertible between right- and left-hand operation.

As the late Vince Marinaro pointed out so frequently, the rod delivers the fly, but it's the reel that fights the fish. Any sort of rod or no rod at all can be employed but hand-holding the line and trying to gather it in and let it go as the fish does its serious fighting is another matter. The practiced hand can, by holding any rod firmly or softly, modulating between the two, handle nearly any size fish if the reel has enough capacity and a properly set drag. Other factors, such as strength of water current, obstacles in and near the water, and a dozen other uncontrollable happenings can have a bearing on the outcome, but the reel is an important mechanical helper. Select yours with care, and it'll serve you a lifetime.

At salmon camps around the world, the name most often heard and imprinted on the reels used is Hardy. It is synonymous with trout- and salmon-fishing gear, and its reputation has been well earned. Some other British makers of fly reels, such as J. W. Young, Farlow, and Cummins, have some loyal fans, but Hardy is the only one of the major British reel makers still producing reels under its own name. The House of Hardy is well into its second century of tackle making. That's a mere eyewink of time when compared with the longevity of some British firms, but it's long enough to have acquired a positive notoriety.

The St. John, St. George, St. Aiden, The Perfect, the LRH, and more recently the Prince and the Marquis are but a few of the model names Hardy has bestowed on its reels. There are and have been many others, but the ones just named have been the salmon stars. I have used them all at one time or another and have never, I repeat, never had a Hardy reel fail me in the heat of battle. My well-traveled St. John, for example, once fell (still attached to the rod) more than ninety feet down the side of a rocky Labrador cliff, bouncing and gathering velocity as it clattered from boulder to boulder. The rod was destroyed, but the reel suffered no more than a few dings and scratches and worked perfectly for the rest of the trip. It still does.

You can buy reels for less money than a Hardy and you can certainly pay more, but a St. John, a salmon-size Perfect, and the newer Marquis with rim control are excellent choices and will match well with ninety percent of the suitable salmon rods made

A J. W. Young Speedex reel. This venerable multiplying reel is a fine example of British crafts-manship. It is a bit heavy for some graphite rods but it has tremendous capacity and carries two hundred yards of thirty-pound backing.

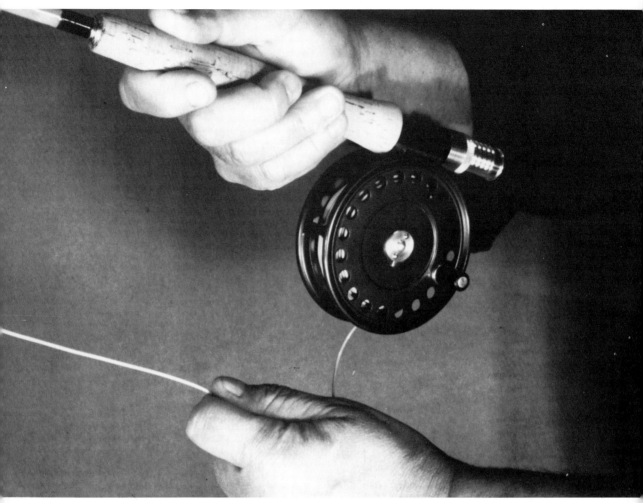

The Hardy St. John is probably the best-known English reel on this side of the Atlantic. Rugged, dependable, and good looking on bamboo or graphite rods, it also has a distinctive click.

A Hardy Perfect model in the wide-spool configuration. This well-known Hardy design has been on the scene for seventy-five years without any major change. Its spool turns on ball bearings, making it the smoothest reel ever conceived.

today. They might be a trifle heavy for a few of the lighter graphite rods but not so much so to cause any great inconvenience. To avoid appearing to be a Hardy shill, I'll stop here, because in today's picture there are so many other great reels, I've got to save some space.

The next Atlantic salmon reel that deserves special mention is the highly reliable Pflueger Medalist. The Medalist, now well over a half-century old, is the best-known fly reel in the United States. Millions of Medalist trout reels in model designations 1494 and 1495 have traveled the streams of the U.S. and Canada, and not a few of them have seen long service in every country where fly rods are waved. I own a well-scarred 1494 that has been involved in forty-two trout seasons and, if the fishing gods please, will see a few more. The much larger 1498 Pflueger has been involved in catching more Atlantic salmon in Canada and the U.S. than all other reels combined. I can't prove that statement with statistical data, but I challenge anyone to prove otherwise.

The Pflueger 1498 is the one most useful reel for Atlantics, but if the river fished is not of awesome size (nor the fish), a 1495½, which has a wider spool than the 1495, is also acceptable. Lack of capacity, however, can create a problem from time to time. One of those times occurred in 1981 when my fishing-crazy wife hooked a magnificent eighteen-pounder on the Mecatina. Yes, she hooked it in the Steady pool, and on the initial run. The hook-beaked cockfish streaked downstream with a vengeance. It stopped only when it ran out of gas, and as I turned toward Sylvia to snap a few pictures of her winding furiously on the reel, I glanced at the spool. There were no more than two wraps of backing remaining! One more wiggle of its broad tail and that salmon would have been gone. She swapped her 1495½ for a 1498 the next day!

The Pflueger is not quite as easily changed from right- to left-hand operation, but it doesn't require a degree in engineering either. The instructions are included with each new reel. With the Hardy-type mechanism it's simply a matter of flopping the triangular-shaped pawl and trading places with the line guard if the reel is equipped with one. While I am a right-handed caster, I switch all of my fly reels to crank from the left. I want to hold my fly rod in the "smart" hand while fighting fish. It's never made any sense to me to switch the rod back and forth when a fish is on the end of the leader doing its best to come unstuck. Some highly intelligent anglers, for whom I have great respect, have stated an opposite case: They want their most dexterous hand doing the cranking. Well, okay, but . . . millions of anglers who are no more intelligent nor coordinated than you and I have no trouble winding their openfaced spinning reels with the left hand. I have the feeling that it's all in how one began. My first fly reel was set up for left-hand retrieve when I swapped a pair of rabbits for it. I never changed. I encourage tyros under my instruction to crank with the left hand, and most continue to do so. But enough about that . . . some of my best friends crank from the right.

At this time, a Pflueger 1498 sells for less than forty dollars at most stores, while

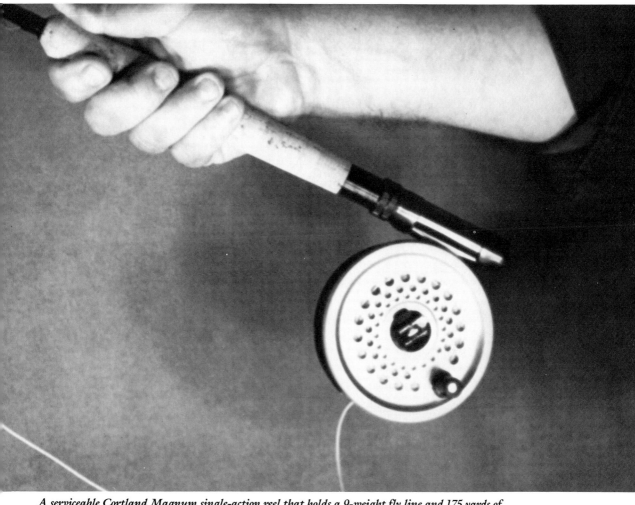

A serviceable Cortland Magnum single-action reel that holds a 9-weight fly line and 175 yards of thirty-pound backing.

the various Hardy models are about three times that much—a factor, of course, for some anglers, but there are plenty of serviceable reels between these prices and some that go much higher. The in-betweeners include the Martin MG-9, an extremely rugged single-action fly reel from a company that's been around since 1884. Scientific Anglers's System II Model 8/9 is in this group at about one hundred dollars and not only works well but looks extremely nice on a black graphite rod. The Cortland SS Magnum at seventy-five dollars is another reel worth considering in the medium price range. It will hold an amazing amount of thirty-pound backing and more twenty-pound backing than one should ever need.

Orvis lists, and has listed over the years, an array of salmon-class reels, with their current Presentation reel and the largest of the CFO series being the best of the group in my opinion. Be sure to get the Presentation reel with the "click." The CFO reels are neat in that no other reel in the world will hold a hundred yards of backing and a full fly line and still weigh less than five ounces. Easy to change the spools, too.

After these, we come to the boutique reels made by custom makers and small manufacturers that are nearly in the custom category. Most of them are first-class products and are nice to own if for no other reason than snob appeal. But there's something to be said about that: snob appeal is not a nice expression—perhaps "pride of ownership" is a better way of putting it. After all, we humans are prideful creatures, particularly those who fish with flies, and we like to show off a bit. It's the same with autos, clothing, firearms, or jogging shoes—it's simply nice to have the nice stuff.

Among the boutique reels, none have the built-in mystique of the Bogdan. Stanley Bogdan of Nashua, New Hampshire, is a perfect example of a cantankerous Yankee craftsman. He makes reels to order only, and makes them and delivers them when he jolly well pleases. His salmon-size reels are mechanical perfection, and if you have several hundred dollars to spare, the wait for one will be worth it. The titled of Europe and the well-heeled in the U.S. and Canada don't consider their angling lives quite complete without a Bogdan reel. These reels do "fish" well, and rigging one's rod with a Bogdan at a salmon camp is bound to elicit envious stares and the assumption that the reel's owner knows a thing or two about salmon fishing. (There are exceptions, however; for example, a good friend of mine owns at least nine Bogdans in various sizes, and he still hasn't learned how to play a fish correctly.)

The Ross reels are sort of boutique class too, but they are certainly more available than Bogdans. The S-2 is a dandy salmon tool except for its being of the silent-drag type. If it only had a click I'd love the S-2, because its drag system, which runs on a brake shoe made from Delrin, is smooth as glass. The Ross is somewhat over three hundred dollars.

If the reel you choose for Atlantic salmon will see extra duty on the salt water, for bonefish, say, or other hard-fighting fish, the reels made for that purpose with corrosion-resistant materials are worth considering. Fenwick's World Class fly reels are in this

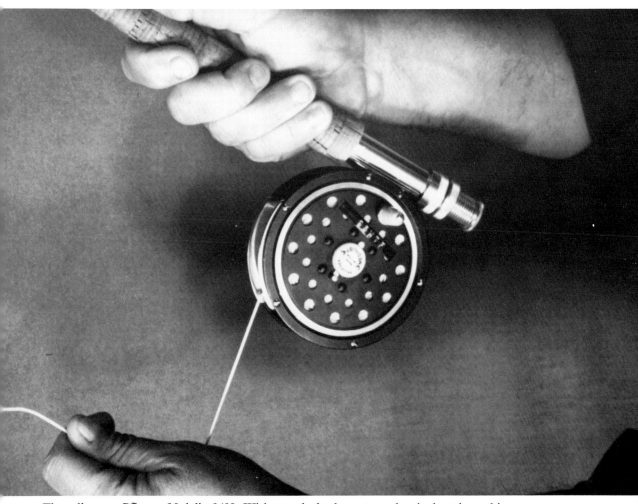

The well-proven Pflueger Medalist 1498. Without a doubt the most popular single-action reel in the United States and Canada.

Orvis CFO reels are English-made and a marvel of simplicity. The author suggests that fly reels be converted to crank from the left side, keeping the "smart" hand on the rod grip at all times.

The interior of an Orvis CFO. By changing the position of the two "dogs" indicated by the pencil points, the reel can be instantly converted from right- to left-hand operation. Most reels with triangular dogs can be changed in the same way.

category, and with sizes suitable for fish from trout to tarpon, they are good buys at slightly over two hundred dollars. At about a hundred dollars more come the Fin-Nor Tycoon reels and the Seamasters. Both of these Florida-made reels were originally built for saltwater fly rodding, but many have seen hard duty on salmon rivers as well. These are the Mack trucks of fly rodding, and nothing short of a nuclear explosion will harm them. Two other Florida reels are the Billy Pate and Catina. Seldom seen in stores outside the Sunshine State, these reels have in a few years proven that they are among the world's best.

There are probably a dozen more small-volume makers out there who deserve mention, but I hesitate to discuss any reel I've never handled. The same holds true with larger makers who are constantly changing and re-engineering their products. If I have a complaint about today's reels, it must be aimed at those manufacturers who are constantly altering a trustworthy design. The best and best-selling fly reels in the world haven't been seriously tinkered with for decades. And the best of the newcomers shouldn't be fooled with either.

The most perplexing observation concerning fly reels is that so many gifted crafts-men develop an uncontrollable desire to make one. The fishing world has not been heavily impacted by the comings and goings of the dozens of designs, sizes, and "innovations" applied to fly reels over the past fifty years. Economically, no one ever got rich making fly reels, and this is especially so in the case of fly reels made solely for salmon or saltwater species. It's got to be labor of love, like fashioning a split bamboo fly rod or building the world's finest kaleidoscope. Make a good reel, and if you do it right, it'll last a lifetime and then some. There isn't much of a repeat market as with razor blades. But then, there will always be a sizable number of fly rodders searching for the perfect reel or "just one more" special-purpose reel that will make their fishing more effective or enjoyable. Come to think of it, there are a couple of empty spaces in my reel drawer that need filling.

6

Lines

Fly lines are so good these days that it would be difficult to declare one absolutely better on all counts than another. The problem of comparison is compounded by the fact that there are only a half dozen or so factories making fly lines, yet there are several dozen brand names appearing on the packages. Some of the very largest of the fly-tackle suppliers don't manufacture the lines bearing their name. I couldn't reveal which company makes so-and-so's line, because such things are shrouded in mystery. But I can guess, and so can you by doing a bit of comparing and feeling. Lines from different makers do feel different, and the one for you is best determined by where you fish and how you cast.

Practically all modern fly lines consist of a braided core of nylon threads tightly woven under a coating of polyvinyl chloride (PVC). By various methods, air bubbles, which one maker calls "microspheres," are trapped in the coating, thus giving a floating line its buoyancy. A decrease in the number of these microspheres allows the line to sink. The outside diameter of the finished line and its overall weight are regulated by the thickness of the coating. The line is sized by pulling it through a forming machine that shapes the line while the PVC coating is still soft. The line then passes through an oven, fusing core to coating and hardening the coating as well.

If you totally understand the foregoing paragraph, you're a light year ahead of me or you are employed by a fly line company. Leon Chandler, executive vice president of Cortland Line Company, would not allow me to photograph the forming process when I visited their factory a few years ago. Leon has been a good friend for many years, but friendship stopped at the edge of "the secret room." And the same situation exists at most other line companies. Well, some things ought to be secret, I guess.

Today's anglers are blessed with a standardized system for determining line size. It's done with numbers with the smaller digit being the smaller in diameter. Today's rod makers followed the lead created by the AFTMA (American Fishing Tackle Manufacturers Association), and most now mark their rods with specific line designations. This system is much easier than it was twenty-five years ago when letters were used, such as HDH, GBF, and so on. The letter system would have been okay except rod makers chose the letters at random and so did those who made lines. The only way to find the right line for a specific rod was to try a bunch of them. This was highly inconvenient if you were dealing through the mail. Furthermore, most graphite, boron, and glass rods are not terribly finicky if they are one size too heavy or too light. They'll cast pretty well with either. Bamboo rods are fussier, and if one is made for an 8 weight line, casting a 9 or 10 will probably overload it.

There are reasons for choosing one line over another for salmon fishing, with casting ability having a lot to do with it. The 444SL line by Cortland has a harder outside coating than any other I've tried. It will not suit the trout fisherman who does a lot of hand-twist retrieving or handles the line a great deal when manipulating wet flies or nymphs. Nor will the 444SL be of any great advantage when casting dry flies less than twenty-five feet. But it is a nearly perfect line for Atlantic salmon fishing or any other situation where longer casts are needed. This is so because the line doesn't "sag" between the guides, and the harder surface allows it to shoot through the guides with less effort. Another line offering similar characteristics is the Orvis SSS floating line. It too has a firm coating that makes extra-distance casting much easier. The premium lines from Scientific Anglers (3M Company) are also first-class products with a slightly "softer" feel, which some anglers prefer. For stripping flies across the surface when a lot of handling is needed, the SA lines are ideal. They are also excellent dry fly lines, since they float like corks and continue to do so with minimal attention. It would be difficult to lay a bad "review" on any of today's fly lines from the companies mentioned or on Berkley, Shakespeare, Garcia, et al. The finishes are good on all of them, and with an occasional cleaning they'll last for a couple seasons of hard fishing.

The line type to be chosen for Atlantic salmon fishing is the weight-forward or WF floating variety. Occasionally a double-taper (DT) floater might be needed for dry fly fishing, but most of the time a WF will do the job. A sink-tip fly line will be useful once in a while when fish are deep and won't respond to flies on or near the surface. Considering the low price of today's quality fly lines, an extra line or two should be carried on all salmon adventures. One of them might as well be a sink-tip. A fast-sinking fly line, while valuable to the Western steelhead angler, will be of little use for Atlantic salmon.

Lee Wulff markets a fly line under his name known as the Triangle Taper. It isn't available in many stores but can be ordered from Lee, Box CC, Livingston Manor, New York 12758. This line is a composite forward-taper with a shooting head that actually is shaped like a long triangle. I don't understand the dynamics of this design, but I am sure about the neat way the line "turns over" on fifty- to sixty-foot casts and still does a decent job at ranges under and over this average distance. His line marked 8–9 casts well on all 9 weight rods I've tried it with.

Some fly fishermen are fussy about the color of their fly line. Across the range of available lines, one can choose just about any color he'd like. They come in peach, white, brown, dark green, mint green, yellow, tan, gray, and fluorescent orange. While there might be some justification for using a line that is less visible to the fish, I've never found line color to be much of a factor. Once on the Miramichi, one of the guides needed a new line. The only spare I had with me that suited his rod was a bright orange one. He admitted that while he had no choice at the moment, he wasn't overjoyed at throwing such a flashy line over Atlantic salmon. He figured it would spook the fish. After two days of being "high rod" and taking some very difficult fish in low water, he became a walking testimonial for bright orange lines. He actually believed the fish were attracted to it!

With a leader nine feet or longer ahead of the fly line, the salmon don't seem to care what color a line is. Except in absolutely dead calm water, fly lines all appear as black silhouettes to the human eye when viewed from beneath the surface. I assume salmon see them in the same way.

Even a small grilse can dash off taking all the fly line on its initial run, requiring a supply of small-diameter backing on the salmon reel. I attach my backing with an Albright knot after stripping some coating from the butt end of the fly line. (See illustration p. 86) Thirty-pound Dacron is the right stuff, and here I am extremely partial to Cortland's product sold under the name Micron. More twenty-pound material can be loaded on a reel than thirty-pound, but the slightly larger diameter is easier to handle. It lays evenly on the reel spool, where twenty-pound has a tendency to cut into itself at inopportune moments. Any material heavier than thirty-pound is wasted space.

7

Leaders

The subject of leaders for fly fishing falls into the same realm of unusual subjectivity as rods. That means that what works well for one may not work for another. If a caster drives his rod forward with a vengeance as the line and leader are delivered, a long, light leader can work well. If the caster makes his toss with less effort, allowing the flex of the rod to do most of the work, he'll need a longer and heavier butt section in his leader to make the cast straighten out nicely. And there are all sorts of techniques in between these extremes. I don't want to make the topic sound that complicated, but explaining it is not unlike describing how to ride a bicycle or do a back flip. The mechanics of either can fill several pages of text, but the raw truth is, you have to *do it* to know how.

The basic leader I use for all of my salmon fishing begins with a piece of monofilament slightly more than thirty inches long. I'm not fussy about the precise measurements of each section in my tapered leaders, since we need a bit of extra to tie the knots. A few inches more or less will not have a great effect on the finished product.

This basic leader, which will total 10.75 feet, is constructed thus:

Length	Diameter	Strength
30 in.	.022 in.	approx. 30-lb. test
15 in.	.020 in.	approx. 25-lb. test
15 in.	.017 in.	approx. 20-lb. test
15 in.	.015 in.	approx. 15-lb. test
24 in.	.013 in.	approx. 12-lb. test
30 in.	.012 in.	approx. 10-lb. test

If I want to fish dry flies or wet flies smaller than size 8, this basic leader is modified by changing the .013 section to fifteen inches, the .012 section to twenty-four inches, and adding a tippet of .010 measuring thirty inches. This change makes a total length of about twelve feet. If one wants to go still finer, the final three sections should be reduced by half and a lighter tippet of thirty inches added.

If the leader you tie or buy doesn't cast well, the first trouble spot to examine or alter is the butt section–the one nearest the line. A longer or heavier butt section will almost always help in "turning over" the leader or causing it to unfurl in a graceful way. Jumping too quickly in a downward direction with leader diameters can also cause strange examples of macramé to occur at the end of a cast. With all fly rods, however, I've found the basic leader works satisfactorily most of the time.

After some practice casting, the ideal prescription that works on your rod should be duplicated; these are the spares you carry in your vest. Ordinarily during fishing, the only repairs needed will be the adding of a tippet, or a tippet and the section next to it. For a full week of fishing, an entire new leader will seldom be called for. But it can happen, and occasionally the way it happens will be memorable. My favorite episode involving lost leaders is one Charlie Fox loves to tell.

For many years Charlie and a small group of pals worked the Little Southwest Miramichi from a fishing shack not far from what was known as the Red Stone Pool. The trail from the camp to the river wound through a dense stand of fir and "jing" weeds; along it a moose was occasionally seen. One morning as Charlie was headed for the river, a young bull with sprouting antlers positioned itself smack in the middle of the narrow path. It showed no desire to move out of the way, so Charlie playfully tapped it on the noggin with the tip of his fly rod. Shocked at this indignity, the moose whirled and took off through the bush at a trot. As it had turned, the tip of one antler had caught on the leader dangling from the rod, and Charlie's reel began to whine as it would when a big fish was hooked. Charlie allowed it was the first time he had ever hooked a moose and stood there in the trail watching his line vanish from the reel spool and wondering what to do next. He decided that the best way to solve the problem was to point the rod at the sound of the moose crashings and hold tight on the reel handle until something broke. He did, and the line parted from the backing with moose taking the leader, fly, and all of the fly line. Moose, line, and leader were never seen again. A most extraordinary way to lose fishing tackle. The biggest laugh of the day occurred later when a New Brunswick guide asked, after Charlie related the story, "What fly did he take?"

As far as spookiness is concerned, Atlantic salmon are not terribly leader shy most of the time. Too much casting and drifting flies over a fish may indeed put it "down" for a time, but I'm convinced it isn't the diameter or length of the leader that creates suspicion. It's simply the continued activity. But a leader of nine feet or more is almost always necessary to get a decent drift over a fish without having the larger-diameter line pulling the fly through the current too swiftly. The leader may not frighten a fish, but a loud plop as the wet fly enters the water or a crashing delivery of a dry fly can reduce the chance of a strike. For these reasons, a leader slightly longer than the normal salmon rod is good practice.

While there are a number of ways to attach a line to a leader, the only two methods today's salmon angler should consider are the nail knot and needle knot. These knots, if tied well, will slip through the guides easily and last for a week of salmon fishing without need for retying.

All leader joints are fashioned with the traditional barrel knot and made with five turns of leader on each side of the knot. Learn to tie this knot and the nail knot and you'll be a happier salmon angler . . . a happier trout angler too. Some tackle suppliers sell finished tapered leaders that are okay for salmon fishing, but I don't trust any knots I didn't tie myself. If I have a knot failure, I know who to blame.

Knotless leaders are also available from a variety of manufacturers and will also work well if the butt portion is heavy enough. It frequently isn't, though, and a piece of heavier material must be tied on to make the leaders cast more efficiently. Then too, as flies are changed a few times, the tippet portion vanishes and a new one or an entire leader must be tied on. I'd rather do it myself from the start. In addition, there is some weird law at work here that confounds me; tapered leaders fashioned from individual sections straighten out better than do the knotless tapers. The hand-tied leaders don't kink and curl as much, and I suspect it's because each knot works like a miniature hinge preventing this. It's another of Murphy's laws that applies to fly casting.

For trout fishing over highly selective trout, a tippet, or at times an entire leader, made from limp leader material is best, but for salmon I'll opt for the hard, stiff variety of monofilament every time. Maxima is the brand I've settled on because it's widely available, takes a knot well, and is sold in that purplish/brown chameleon color. I like the color simply because it's about the shade of the water in many Canadian rivers. Water flowing through the conifer stands of the maritime provinces takes on a reddish brown hue, and Maxima matches it perfectly. Clear monofilament seems to work as well, so I suppose my preference is mostly a matter of hair-splitting.

I am sure, however, that using monofilaments containing fluorescent dyes can reduce the likelihood of a strike. These materials are highly visible and when tied to a

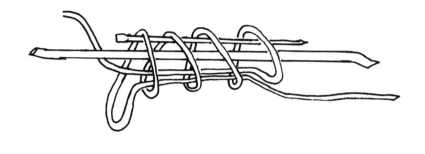

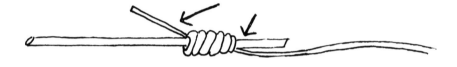

Nail knot

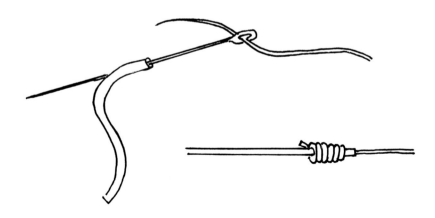

Needle knot

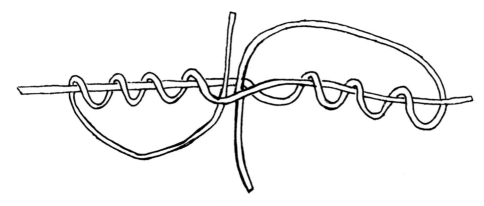

Blood knot

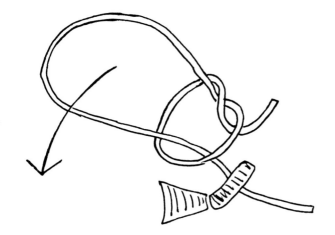

Turle knot

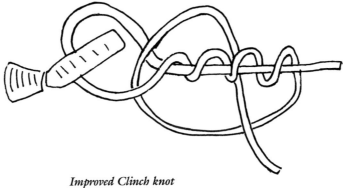

Improved Clinch knot

fly can spook salmon. One morning on the Eagle River I watched three different fish rise confidently to a fly and turn abruptly away at the last second from a shiny tippet. The same three fish were hooked two hours later when presented the *same* fly on a non-fluorescent leader. I'm a believer.

There are two tried and true knots that are the universal choices for attaching single-hook flies. One is the Turle and the other is the Improved Clinch. The Turle is preferred by those who insist that their fly ride straight in the water and not cocked up or down as happens with the Improved Clinch. Most knots other than the Turle will not hold the fly straight if up-turned hooks are used. Since the majority of salmon flies are tied on up-eyed hooks, this presents a bit of a dilemma. The Turle knot is not as strong as the Improved Clinch, so the angler is faced with the choice of having his fly ride straight or using the stronger knot. In practice it matters little, since a heap of salmon have been caught with both knots, and rarely does either fail if tied well.

The Riffle Hitch, or Portland Hitch, which I use a great deal, can be added after a Turle or Improved Clinch knot. Tying it consists of looping the leader over the fly with two half hitches and drawing it up tight behind the head of the fly. This forces the wet fly to plane on the surface like a tiny surfboard. You'll read more about the hitch later on.

The Turle knot can be used to attach double-hook flies when their use is called for, but I prefer a variation of the girth hitch, generally termed the guide's knot. This provides a double wrap of leader material around the eye of the hook and when tightened holds double hooks in a rigid, upright position.

I used to tie loops in the end of my line (after stripping the coating from the final eight inches) and interlock that to another loop in the backing. I stopped doing this a few years back when one of the loops somehow got caught on the tip of a favorite rod. The resulting mess broke rod tip, lost the fish, and fractured my composure. I continue to strip off some fly line coating (using a girth hitch of fifteen-pound mono and peeling it off) and tie the uncoated fly line to the backing with an Albright knot. I've never had this knot fail with a fish, although I do retie it at the beginning of each week of fishing.

If you learn the knots mentioned, you'll be equipped for any freshwater situation. Take the time to do it and you'll be surprised at how many fellow anglers come to you for assistance. It will become a matter of pride to know that you can tie them well.

Observations on Knot Tiers

Outdoor writers are usually quite good at tying fishing knots—they'd appear mighty foolish if they didn't because they write about knots with such annoying regularity. Physicians (with few notable exceptions) don't tie knots well. They all think they do, but apparently the task is too mundane for them. Attorneys can't tie their

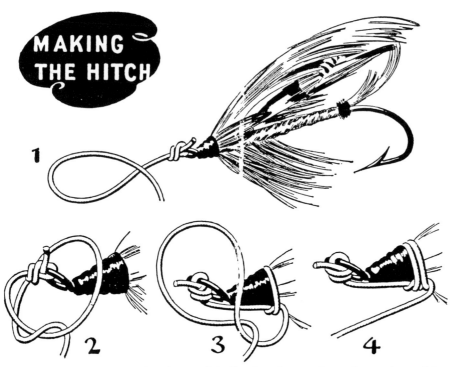

Put a loop in the leader just in advance of the fly, throw it up and over the eye, then pull it tight to form an overhand knot around the shank of the hook at the base of the head. Then do a repeat, tightening the second knot just beyond the first. (Courtesy Outdoor Life)

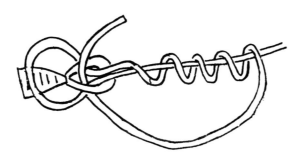

Guides knot

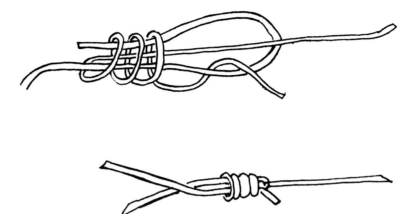

Albright knot

shoes without help. Curiously, bankers are very good at knots. The absolute best knot tiers, as a profession, are dentists. I have yet to meet a dentist who cannot master the most intricate of knots. If dentists choose to tie flies, they are extremely good at it. (These revelations have probably cost me some referral sales among M.D.'s and the legal profession, but I hope every dentist in the world will want to quote from this chapter.)

8

Playing, Landing, and Releasing

Assuming that you have read the chapter titled "How They Are Fished," and understand the advice given and apply it, a salmon should become attached to your fly eventually. The coiled energy packed into a smallish grilse will astound the first-timer and that of a full-bodied fish of twelve pounds or more can be frightening.

A few seasons ago, when coaching a salmon "virgin" on his first turn through a favorite pool on the lovely little Mecatina River, I made the boastful remark that I'd hooked over a hundred fish from the exact spot he was casting to. The beginner made the observation that in that case it must be "old hat," that watching him couldn't be very exciting, and that my hooking another fish would be just more of the same. As I was assuring him that every fish was a new adventure, his line went tight with a solid pull, and a beautiful bright salmon bolted into the air. While talking him through the proper way to handle his fish, I made an attempt to remain very cool to keep the novice angler's excitement meter at a controllable level. To his great credit, he didn't foul up the procedure, and after a fine show of running and leaping, the fish was netted cleanly by our guide. "Pretty exciting, huh?" I shouted as I tapped a cigarette out of the pack and reached into the wader pocket for the lighter.

"The greatest," he beamed. "But be careful, Jim. You've already got a cigarette in your mouth!"

And so I had. So much for being cool.

The foregoing incident is a perfect illustration of how the hooking and playing of an Atlantic salmon can affect observer or participant. Some generalities can be said of all salmon that find a hook in their jaws, but each one can react differently and just as sure as night follows day, a fish will break the rules at the precise moment you decide to make a profound statement on the subject. But for a few paragraphs, please extend the courtesy of allowing me to go through the motions of how most fish *do* respond to the hook; well, about fifty percent of them.

The realization that some outside force has them by the nose comes quickly to small salmon (the grilse) and not so quickly to fish of ten pounds or more. It may be that the larger fish is surer of its ability to get away and not quite so concerned at the outset of the angler-fish battle. The grilse usually shakes its head a time or two and then streaks off in the direction its head is pointed at the time. In some pools there seems to be an upstream or downstream preference for the initial run, but I honestly think the direction has more to do with the way fish take the fly at a particular location. Whichever way the most open stretch of water lies seems to be the direction they choose. A larger fish will usually do some of this headshaking too, a sort of shrugging of the shoulders in an attempt to shake the annoyance free. In fact, this tug-tug-tug feeling transmitted through the line into the hand holding the rod may go on for several seconds before a big fish makes his first run. Eventually, all but the odd fish will make a blazing run.

This is the first critical period of the engagement. If you have some loose coils of line about your person, on the water, or between your legs, those coils can do tricks through the rod guides while trying to follow the running salmon. If the line clears nicely, the squeal of the reel is a comforting sound. If the sound of the reel *isn't* heard, the next sound will be the crack of leader breaking or a volley of unprintable words. Sometimes both. Even men of the cloth have been reduced to less than polite language at such times. The best plan here is to watch the slack line and make the necessary moves while trying to avert disaster.

While stripping line or otherwise gathering slack around the wader tops, the experienced angler always keeps a corner of his eye on its whereabouts. If there is some current where you're standing, as there usually is, try to keep the slack line in front of the legs so it hangs in loose loops in a downstream direction. When a fish is struck and begins its run, it's much easier to guide line through the stripping guide (the one nearest the grip) until it comes tight on the reel. Allow the slack to slide through a circle formed with thumb and forefinger of the off hand, without putting much pressure on the line. This is a tricky thing to do and, like riding a bicycle, can't be described in print. It's strictly a "feel" operation, but after you've done it a time or three, you'll know just how much pressure to apply. The correct amount of pressure is that which allows the line to slide through the guides without whipping back or backlashing into a strange knot.

A freshly hooked salmon of any size simply cannot be held tight if it has the chance to shake its tail three times, putting it into full flight. Its frantic efforts will either tear the hook loose, break the leader, or something else. The angler who "freezes" with one hand locked on the rod grip and the other on the reel handles will never hang onto a salmon. If the reel handle begins to turn, which it usually does, fingers and knuckles anywhere near it are bound to get rapped and possibly broken. Salmon fishing is not really a dangerous sport, but a reel handle turning at blurring speed is impossible to stop. Don't even try. As long as the fish is running, keep your hands away from the outside of the reel. If you see you're running out of backing or that the fish is about to get into a dangerous location behind a boulder or chunk of driftwood, the only way to apply additional drag is to touch (lightly) with one finger the backside of the reel spool—or the edge of a rim-control reel. The best plan is to set the drag on your reel at a spot that is slightly above overrun speed. A steady pull on a ten-pound leader simply won't break it when the pull is exerted by a fly rod. You'd have to jerk smartly or get a nearly straight pull to do it by hand. A fish, however, can exert a tremendous pull when running with the current, or by flinging its weight against a leader as it leaps. Drag on a salmon reel is important, very important, but it should never be overly tight.

When a fish punctuates its run with leaps greyhound fashion in the direction of its flight, it's difficult to lower the rod quickly enough. "Bowing" to the fish is how the right response is usually described. But when a fish jumps as it runs, the action is usually too fast for most anglers to do precisely the right thing. As the fish settles down a bit after the first run, there is a kind of trembling sensation that comes through the line into the rod hand that indicates another jump is coming. No kidding; it can be anticipated more often than not. To the beginner it appears that a leap happens too fast for an ordinary mortal to plan a counteraction—but there is time.

As the fish clears the water, lower the rod tip to release the tension to avoid a sudden shock as the fish flops end-for-end in the air. A tight hold on a fish in the air can cause it to come unstuck in a hurry, even with a solid hook hold. The full weight of the fish jerks at the hook and out it comes. Slack line given at the right microsecond avoids the direct pull. Then, as soon as the fish is back in the water, snug up with the rod tip and reel in any slack quickly to come tight once more.

Many times a fish will jump quickly, almost instantly, upon being hooked, before shooting off. This first quick jump can catch the angler off guard, so be ready for it. If there is time after feeling the fish solidly, reel up slack line and get the "fish on the reel." Let the moderate drag of the reel do the work, and don't try to horse the fish with the

A big salmon boils for a hitched fly and is hooked. The next second will see the fish bolting away on its initial run. Don't touch that reel handle at this point!

This leaper caught the angler with his rod too high in the air. Proper rod handling in this situation calls for the rod to be lowered or bowed to the fish. Easing off on the tension prevents the weight of the fish from breaking the leader.

rod. From a mechanical point of view, the salmon should be fought with the reel and not the rod. The rod becomes much more important at the tail end of the battle when the tiring salmon can be led into the net or into position for tailing or beaching.

As an easy-to-follow plan of attack, I recommend that the novice try to keep his rod tip pointed at an imaginary spot about fifteen degrees from vertical toward the fish. At this attitude, the reel will release line when the fish runs and keep enough tension on it to bring about fatigue when the fish doesn't. Reel in when the fish permits it, allow it to run when it must, and the battle will be over in about five minutes for a grilse and in slightly more than a minute per pound for larger salmon. These figures will vary with heft of the leader used, stiffness of the rod, and the sort of pool playing host to the action. The fish itself can be a factor: A bright salmon new to the fresh water can run like a demon and jump like a kangaroo. In terms of time required to land it, such a fish will knock itself out quicker than a sullen sulker that refuses to do much more than choose a place in the current behind a rock and try to stay there. But please remember what I said about profound statements—they seldom are.

The first run will always be the strongest, if not the longest, and each run will diminish in power until the fish is reduced to making circles of decreasing circumference. When it begins to show some flash of white belly, it's time to start thinking about the end of the battle. Now is when the rod takes on special importance.

The fish is tired and can actually be led to a vantage point for netting, beaching, or tailing. Watch carefully to see where the fly is situated in the salmon's mouth. Knowing where you stood when the fish was hooked will generally be a clue as to which side of the jaw the hook is stuck. Try not to exert much pressure on the opposite side. If you do this, the hook can be easily pulled out of the wound, which increased in size during the fracas. Thousands of salmon have been lost at nearly the end of the battle because of a clumsy jerk (person or movement) or sudden switch of rod position. When the fish is close, keep a sharp eye on where the leader ends at the jaw line, and you'll know which way to adjust the position of the tip to apply steady pressure at the right angle. Pay careful attention to the knot where leader joins line. At the end of the fight, this knot may go back and forth through the tip-top and upper guides several times, and a smooth connection here is critical. A sudden foul-up can lose a fish quickly if a final rush for freedom catches you napping. If possible, try to keep the knot out of the guides and direct the person doing the netting to a position where this can be accomplished.

If the fish is to be netted by someone other than you, it's hoped that it will be done by one who's done the job before. Experienced guides know that sudden movements and herky-jerky moves at this point seldom result in success. The best way is to keep the net in the water and lead the fish over it, picking up smartly and cleanly with one smooth stroke. Slashing and jabbing in a frantic manner is bad form and almost

The end of the battle arrives as the fish is led into the waiting net. Slashing and jabbing with the net is bad form and a sure way to lose fish. When the net bow goes past the fish's head, allow the line to go slack.

always causes trouble: the leader can be struck, and a well-worn hook hold will invariably come loose. Sometimes we get lucky, and I can't count the times I've seen fish flopping in the net only to see them flop out and swim away—the hook simply dropped out when the tension was released!

Guides on rivers where a greater percentage of the salmon taken are seven pounds or larger are usually better at handtailing. They've simply had more experience. Some of them can handtail a grilse—until you've tried this maneuver, you haven't known frustration. The problem is, a grilse's tail hasn't yet developed the hard top and bottom rays that form the stiff "fan" of an adult salmon's caudal (tail) fin. Pressure can be applied to the small "wrist" of the body just ahead of the tail, if you have a large strong hand, but it isn't easy. If a grilse is to be killed for consumption, netting is preferred. If the grilse is to be released, slide the hand down the leader until you are within an inch or two of the jaw, and twist or shake the hook free. Ninety-five percent of the time it will snap out easily. If it won't, and if you're serious about not injuring the fish, cut the leader with your clippers or pocket knife and say good-bye to the fly. It will be dislodged or rust out in a short time.

A fish of seven pounds or more can be tailed with a handtailer device or by hand, with the latter method much preferred for two reasons. The metal tailer, even if the cable is plastic-coated, can injure a fish, particularly a very large one if it thrashes or if it's lifted clear of the water for pictures or transport to the beach. If the fish is to be killed, this doesn't matter; but if release is desired, and the flesh is damaged, spine injured, or too many scales knocked loose, the fish may not survive. Handtailing is much easier on the fish, and the satisfaction of doing it is tremendous. It puts the angler into the contest in a most pronounced way.

A person with a large hand and long fingers has a tremendous advantage in tailing a salmon. To do it best requires that the fingers encircle the entire "wrist" of the tail and bring thumb pressure on the point where flesh meets upper tail ray. I've seen persons skilled at tailing grab a fish with the thumb on the bottom of the tail and facing the head of the fish—but this doesn't work out well for most who try it. It's far better to work the fish into a position where its tail is pointed toward the angler and slowly to wrap the hand around the rear portion of the body with thumb on top. Smoothly and firmly, with a forceful increase of pressure, squeeze and lift at the same time. Steady pressure on the junction point between ray and flesh will immobilize the fish and allow it to be lifted free of the water and high enough to prevent it from wig-wagging free. As soon as possible if pictures are to be taken, put your rod down or hand it to someone. Support the fish's heavy belly with the other hand, and you'll be amazed at how docile a big salmon can be.

Finish the photo session as quickly as possible, for two reasons: The fish will never look better than it will at this moment with its eyes still bright and flanks gleaming; the person holding the fish will never look happier, and the expression on his face or her

A twelve-pound salmon is securely in the net. The angler hasn't yet allowed the line to go slack, which he should, in order to prevent a freed fly from sticking himself or the guide. Get to the shoreline for pictures!

face won't be "acting." If the fish is to be released (as currently all large salmon must be in several provinces of Canada), an additional third reason applies: The fish will have a much better chance of swimming away relatively unhurt instead of being in jeopardy by having spent too much time out of water.

I must admit that some of my early attempts at handtailing were not exactly moments of grace. One of the most memorable sequences of salmon-grabbing took place on the Hunt River five seasons ago in the presence of a guide named Sonny and my good pal Jack Wise of Exton, Pennsylvania. Jack is an accomplished salmon angler with many seasons notched on his rod and a delight to be with. His sense of humor and love of the game make him a nice addition to any trip. This time, I wanted to utilize him as a photographer while I performed what I hoped would be a textbook example of how to tail a sixteen-pound salmon. The fish performed well, and as I led it into an eddy of calm water, I was explaining to Jack what I wanted in the way of photos.

"Now Jack, try to get a shot when I reach into the water, and then one as I first lift the fish up and then . . . so on and so on." I was directing like C. B. de Mille, and Jack had his face glued on the eyepiece of the motor-driven 35mm. Everything was coming together nicely as I reached for the fish, when suddenly the rock under my left foot slipped, and the fish reacted by making a last dash—and swam between my legs!

In holding the fish quietly for a few seconds while setting up the scene, I had allowed it to regain some gusto. It tore off for ten feet and actually made a leap behind me. The tip and half the center section of my graphite rod was now between my legs with a loop of line wrapped around one leg and my right hand. How all this happened in about one-hundredth of a second is impossible to explain, but it did, and fortunately the salmon fanned calmly for a full minute while I untangled myself. Reeling the fish back into position for the photographer was quickly accomplished, and now I was ready for a second try. "Okay, Jack, let's try it again."

I looked for Jack, who had been standing on a rustic wooden casting platform, and he was on his back rolling with laughter. I wasn't too amused, and I yelled, "Come on, be serious, I really want this sequence of pictures."

He got into position again, still chuckling, and at that moment, my wader suspenders decided to come loose, and they fell to half-mast, causing another delay. The fish wiggled and lay still, thank goodness. Waders hitched up, I reached down as calmly as I could and neatly snatched the fish from the water.

"Okay, now do it again," Jack said. "I got the shot all right, but I'd like to take another just to be sure."

I lowered the fish into water gently and relaxed my grip just slightly to relieve a muscle spasm, planning to regrip quickly. To my utter amazement, the fish swam away at a slow, dignified pace and vanished into the depths of the pool. It had been unhooked at least three minutes!

Six of the best-known classic Atlantic salmon flies are in the left column and their hairwing counterparts are on the right. They are, from top to bottom: Thunder and Lightning, Jock Scott, Green Highlander, Dusty Miller, Blue Charm, and Durham Ranger. While the classics are beautiful, the hairwings are more widely used. They are less expensive to make and more durable. Some may argue that the salmon know the difference, but in practice, it doesn't seem to matter.

In the author's opinion the six most popular classic flies of all time. Vertically on the left: *Jock Scott, Dusty Miller, and Durham Ranger.* On the right from the top: *Thunder and Lightning, Green Highlander, and Blue Charm.*

The flies from the previous photo, but tied as hairwings, without the fancy feathers in the wing.
The jungle cock cheeks are there, however, adding a touch of elegance.

Six popular flies for Maine rivers, but they've proven their worth elsewhere as well. **From top to bottom, left row:** *Wringer, Cosseboom, Colburn Special.* **Right row from top to bottom:** *Turk, Blue Charm, Pink Ent.*

The author's favorite salmon fly is the Mar Lodge, shown here in five variations. At top left is J. Edson Leonard's version—a racy style indeed! At top right is Maine tier Bob Ent's slim edition. Ent's traditional Mar Lodge is in the center, complete with twisted-gut eye. The bottom two are by the author with apologies to Leonard, Ent, Kelson, and Pryce-Tannent!

Stunning examples of the fly tier's art, as executed by Bob Ent of Bangor, Maine. The yellow-winged dandy at top left is a Colonel Bates and is certainly bright enough to "light the salmon's journey." Top right is Evening Star, featuring four pairs of matched jungle cock eyes the length of the body. Lower left is Lady Amherst, a simple but elegant pattern. Bottom right is the Orange Parson. There are no insect counterparts for such creations and we must assume that when these patterns were created, the tiers were designing for the human eye only.

The Bomber. Some purists declare it isn't really a fly but a bass bug masquerading as a salmon fly. Whatever it's called, the worth of this fuzzy creation on salmon rivers in Canada and the U.S. has been well proven over the past twenty years. The largest here is tied on a size 4 long-shank hook. The other two are dressed on 6s—one long shank and the other of regular length. Although Bombers of all colors have taken salmon, brown, white, and combinations of these seem to work best.

The famous Rats. Rusty Rat, at the top, is the best known of the group, which is characterized by an extension of floss extending from the front half of the body—the "tail." Most rats also wear peacock-sword-feather tails, and while the original wing calls for silver monkey, grey-fox back hair works just as well. The Silver Rat is on the left and the Blue Rat is at the bottom. All three have caught fish here and abroad. The Blue Rat is especially productive in Iceland. All are perfectly tied by Bob Ent of Bangor, Maine.

A typical box of Atlantic salmon flies that could be found in an angler's kit on any river in the world. Since the Atlantic salmon is not a freshwater feeder the novice will ask "Why carry so many different patterns?" Salmon merely react to a fly pattern, they don't get involved in rational thinking. If a certain fly does the job, well, that's the one it wanted on that particular day. The next fish may choose something else.

The Royal Wulff, the most famous salmon dry fly in the world and one of Lee Wulff's many contributions to the game.

The Royal Lee, a classic salmon fly tied on the occasion of Lee Wulff's 1983 testimonial dinner at the Anglers' Club of New York.

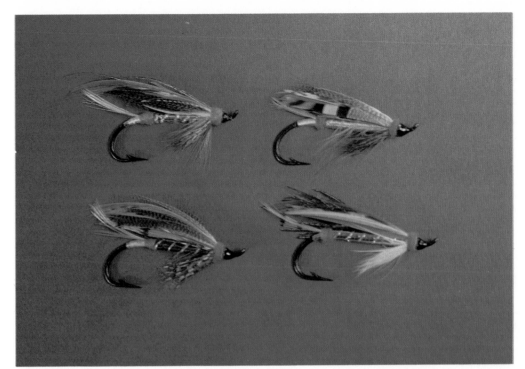

The Doctor series of classics. Top row left to right: *Silver Doctor, Blue Doctor.* Second row left to right: *Black Doctor, Helmsdale Doctor. The Doctor patterns are at least one hundred years old and all have caught salmon wherever they have been fished. The Silver Doctor is by far the most famous pattern, but the author believes the Black Doctor is a better producer.*

This version of a caddisfly is one of the author's favorites on broken water. A down-wing fly can be "scooted" on the surface and will sometimes bring a strike when nothing else works.

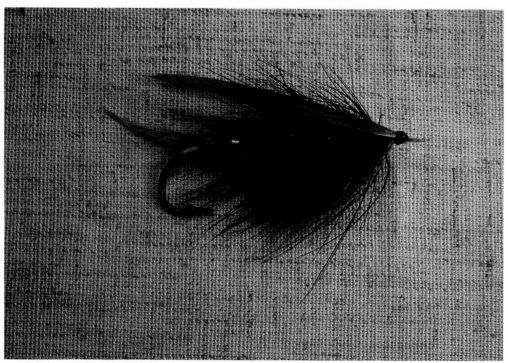

A perfect example of a Dee-Strip salmon fly, as tied by Helen Shaw. This is the Glentanna pattern pictured in Pryce-Tannent's book and is a precise duplicate right down to the twisted-gut eye.

An ancient Jock Scott tied by an unknown Scottish tier well before 1900. This fly was undoubtedly tied without a vise.

The scruffy and ugly Bombers. These deer-and-caribou-hair creations are great salmon attractors and will locate a fish that might not rise for anything else. Very popular in Labrador and Newfoundland, they've also caught salmon everywhere else.

The Curt Hill Haystack is a new favorite and will bring salmon to the surface with amazing results in smooth water. The fly body rides flat on the water and is easy to hook with because no hackle points get in the way.

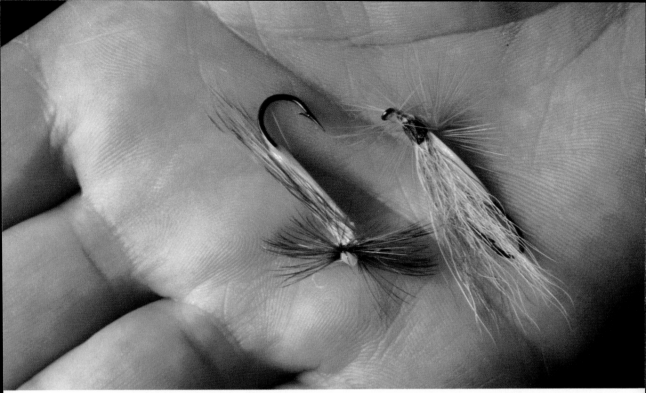

Lee Wulff's Surface Stone Flies are made with Lee's patented molded body. This fly can be fished wet or dry.

A bright fish deserves to be photographed with bright flowers.

Top left: *Sylvia Bashline with a fine cock fish that weighed nearly eighteen pounds. When this fish was hooked it ran well over 150 yards before making its first jump. Sylvia is much happier than the fish.*

Bottom left: *Jack Samson with a twenty-pound George River salmon that fell for a Black Dose.*

Top right: *Sylvia casts into Camp Pool Two on the Mecatina while the guide watches the salmon she has her sights on. Such observations can teach a lot about salmon reactions to different flies and techniques. One caution: If you're in the tree, don't holler too loudly when a fish heads for the fly. The angler may be frightened!*

An attempt to tail this salmon goes amiss, but the Icelandic guide will have another crack at it—and he'll get it.

A beautiful cock fish on the Hunt River that was undone by the dry fly in the hinge of its jaw. This fish rose five times before being hooked.

A fine fourteen-pound Icelandic salmon from the Longa River. Guides in Iceland disdain the net and insist on handtailing whenever possible. They're better at it than any other guides in the world.

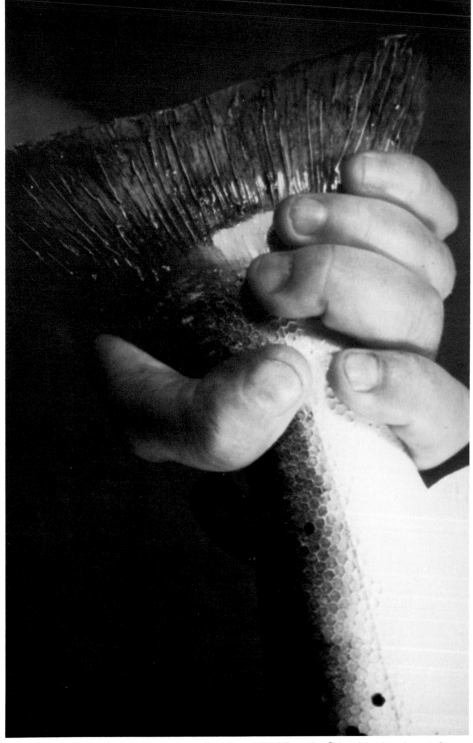

The proper grip for handtailing an adult salmon. Holding the fish with thumb and fingers pressing on the "wrist" of the tail does not cause injury to the fish if it is to be released.

Wise didn't stop laughing for three hours. Somehow we're still friends.

Beaching a salmon is not any easier than netting it, even where a beach of sand or gravel eases into the water at a convenient angle. If you've ever tried to lead a head-strong pup on a long leash, you've got some idea of what it's like to coax a salmon into extremely shallow water. Unless salmon are quite spent, they don't like the feel of gravel on their bellies while they're hooked through the snout at the same time. This is not a job for the faint of heart or a frayed leader. It's much easier with a grilse than with an adult salmon, but the system is the same.

As the tail strikes the beach the fish will cartwheel and flop. Each time it flops, part of its weight or perhaps all of it is against a taut leader. The idea is to keep backing up with a long arc in the rod. Each time the fish makes a move, increase the pull and move to the rear. This maneuver is best done with all of the leader and five or six feet of line. Too short a hold on the fish, and the chance of the full weight of the salmon pulling on the rod tip can cause too much strain. Once you get him sliding and flopping, don't stop until the fish is on solid ground. Obviously, this is far too rough on any fish you choose to release. Plan your meals and count your salmon tags well before trying a beach landing!

The uncompromising gaff was much used in Canada several years ago and is still the capturing instrument of choice on some British and European rivers. It has no place in today's salmon angling picture because of the matter of returning adult fish by law or choice. I've seen salmon gaffed, and gaffed a couple myself–but will not do it again. When done correctly, the gaff not only secures the fish but kills it as well. When done incorrectly, it wounds, and may knock the fish free in the process and the fish dies anyway. With large ocean species that have the teeth and jaw power to maim or kill human beings, there is certainly justification for the gaff. Salmon, however, are no threat in themselves. The gaff for Atlantic salmon should be retired everywhere.

Special Fish-Fighting Situations

It is fairly common for an adult salmon to sulk or hug the bottom in an annoying way that allows such a fish to conserve his energy, seemingly forever. The battle is won by forcing the fish to run, jump, and charge about, sapping its strength with every move. When a fish won't do this, it seems to the novice rod holder that that's all he is– just someone standing there holding the rod with a bend in it, waiting for something to happen. Even the occasional grilse will pick a spot in the current and stay there until the river freezes. A fish like this must be forced to move or you will be there for more time than you might imagine. A big fish can set its fins and absorb a tremendous amount of hauling without moving an inch.

If the fish is in water approachable in waders, sometimes a few steps toward it will start it moving. I've thrown stones at them and prodded them with sticks and paddles

The angler here is attempting to beach a salmon by walking backward and forcing the fish to flop onto the beach. Such landing techniques can work if steady pressure is applied each time the fish moves.

but don't advise doing this anymore. I fell out of a canoe once trying to prod a fish into action. A far better way is to change the angle on the line and leader from front to back and side to side—not violently, mind you, but enough to create some action at the entry point of the hook. A fish can't take too much of this annoying movement and will try to get away from it. Once you get him moving, keep it up and apply slightly more pressure with the rod hand. Once it begins to act like a proper salmon—running and jumping—you'll tire him in short order.

If you are sure a fish is hooked lightly in the tip of the snout or by a mere slip of lip skin, you'll be worried about the fish jumping. It doesn't always work, but by keeping the rod at near right angles to the surface of the water, pulling to the side instead of up, the fish is less likely to jump. When doing this, be sure you know where your guide or fishing partner is. I once saw a lovely Hardy bamboo rod stepped on while this low rod trick was being demonstrated. The poor guide was so intent on watching the fish that he took a step forward and neatly cracked the rod at the tip ferrule. Salmon fishing comes loaded with strange happenings!

With a fish that is about to plunge over a falls or into a white-water froth where you can't follow, there are only two worthwhile actions. Reel back hard, hoping everything stays together (it usually doesn't); or allow the line to go slack and hope the salmon figures the annoyance is gone and swims back into the pool. The latter trick works more often than you might guess. It is a natural reaction for the salmon to pull against the tug of the fly. If a "button hook" of line is created by drifting the line below the fish, the pull comes from downstream instead of up. And up comes the fish to a more manageable position, and the angler breathes easier. This situation frequently happens by accident when a salmon races downstream in an otherwise open pool. As the fish pulls more line from the reel, a natural loop forms on the water until there is a pull coming from right angles, or below the fish. As if by magic, the fish you thought was headed for the ocean turns to return close to where it was hooked. This is simply a salmon's desire to come back to the lie it chose as a resting place. It's a temporary home for the fish and it feels comfortable there. Keep tabs on how often a fish is netted at a location close to the spot where it was hooked. It happens more frequently than not.

The advice given by many experienced salmon anglers for fighting a fish is to try and place yourself at right angles or slightly downstream from it to apply maximum pressure. So situated, the rod pulls with the help of the current, forcing the fish to put forth extra effort. Good advice, as far as it goes, but there are times when this technique works against the angler. If the pool ends quickly and falls or serious rapids are immediately downstream, applying too much pressure may force a fish to give up quickly and make a desperation move down and out of the pool, and is perhaps gone forever.

Getting too close to the fish and having a short line on him when he's still full of energy can also cause panic. Keeping the fish in the pool is the main objective. At times this is best done by easing up a bit on the rod and walking upstream in an attempt to "lead" the fish away from trouble. Believe it or not, this can be done with the majority of salmon if you move slowly and keep a light but even tension on the line. As long as the fish's belly or fins won't touch the bottom and its back is covered as well, a salmon can be coaxed along with a steady hand. A sudden jerk or too much pressure will foul up the procedure, but I've successfully led fish for a hundred yards or more to a better netting or tailing location.

I first saw this trick performed while watching an unknown angler hook large salmon in the "town pool" in the village of Matane, Quebec. The big fish was hooked at the very lip of the pool, and if it turned downstream, it would most likely be lost in the fast water. As soon as the fish was attached, the angler began to walk upstream along the edge of the quieter portion of the pool. He kept his rod low and bent just enough to put very mild pressure on the fish. When first hooked, the fish had wallowed a bit, done some head shaking, and then just resumed its position. With no great amount of pressure on it, the fish apparently didn't realize it was in jeopardy. As he walked the fish up and away from trouble, it would occasionally turn and head for the lip of the pool. But the angler expertly eased up and allowed a loop of line to drift in the current, creating the impression that the pull was coming from downstream. The salmon would turn to face the current, and the angler would resume the gentle persuasion. The battle became a bit more spirited when more pressure was applied to get on with the show, but each time the fish would turn downstream, it would be gently coerced back into the safe water. Eventually, the angler waded into the water up to his thighs and snatched the fish with a perfect handtailing job. It was a masterful performance and one I never forgot.

The "minute-to-the-pound" theory is a good rule of thumb, but some fish simply aren't aware of it. It seems to work perfectly with grilse of six pounds or less. When a fish reaches the ten-pound mark, however, strange things can happen. Some fish are simply stronger than others, and some fish are just plain quitters. The type of water a fish is hooked in can certainly make a difference and, of course, so can the attitude and skill of the angler.

From the tiniest trout in the world to the largest species caught on rod and reel, there is a vast difference in the amount of sheer muscle power required from the angler to effect capture. Yet armed with the right tackle, a seventy-five-pound human can whip a four-hundred-pound marlin in short order. It can be done because the fish literally kills itself by running and jumping. The less a fish jumps, the more difficult it is to land. Tuna, groupers, jacks, and many of the sharks seldom jump and for that reason put on prolonged underwater battles that are taxing on tackle and angler. Salmon that don't jump are always more difficult to land than are those that put on a great show. Personally, I like to see them jump. It's part of the thrill of salmon fishing.

Aside from how a fish fights in a visible way, I firmly believe there is metaphysical force at work every time a fish is hooked. Perhaps a new word is in order here:

This fish is headed for the fast water, and the best way to keep it in the pool is to walk slowly upstream, keeping a firm but steady hand on the rod. If this fails, allow the line to go slack, thus causing the current to pull on the slack from the downstream side.

metapiscatorial. I like that. It suits the issue much better than any existing word, because no other connotes the bond that forms between angler and fish during a prolonged struggle. The successful outcome of the contest from the angler's point of view is a bad happening for the hooked fish. The worst of these happenings is death. In the case of Atlantic salmon and a few other species that are occasionally the recipients of human kindness, a reasonably gentle release is the best of happenings. I'm sure the fish don't consider any of this. (And it's doubtful even if the warm-blooded vertebrates other than man have any understanding of death.) They do, though, seem to know there is a need to flee from the human form, and certainly show panic in doing so at times. Like the reactionary reflexes that goad salmon to rise and intercept a fly, an inner signal warns the fish when a hook is at last realized as something that won't go away. The strange force on the other end of the gossamer strand that checks its escape means serious trouble.

From the angler's end of the tackle, experience cannot be overemphasized. But there is something in the genes or the magnetic field or whatever of each individual that is capable of establishing a bond between him and the fish. When making love, reaching the summit of a mountain, or rolling a seven when we've decided to shoot the bankroll in craps, we feel a "high" that we enjoy and may even understand for a fleeting moment–but we can't explain it to others. I sincerely believe that similarly, during a prolonged battle between human and fish, a mental linkage occurs, and if the angler is tuned to the right frequency, he'll know when it happens.

Anglers who work the ocean's blue water for the behemoths of the fish world, the tuna, the swordfish, marlin, and sharks the size of automobiles, are much more aware of this mental hook-up between man and fish than are freshwater anglers. There is a large measure of physical strength involved here, but whipping one of these monsters is easier by far if you *think* you can do it, thereby convincing the fish it's on the losing end of the fight. When a number of well-traveled big game anglers were quizzed, they all admitted to *knowing precisely* the moment during a fish fight when the tide had shifted in their favor. They know when the fish has reached the give-up stage and react with extra effort to bring the contest to a swift conclusion. To a man or woman, they all agree that each fish demonstrates a different degree of courage or "heart" that has little or nothing to do with its size. A four-hundred-pound marlin, for example, might fight much longer and harder than one weighing eight hundred pounds. And it is the same with Atlantic salmon. I've seen twelve-pound fish worry an angler for sixty minutes or longer when not pressured enough and twenty-five-pounders give up the ghost in less than fifteen.

In winning against any fish, the secret is constant, unrelenting pressure modulated only by a smooth blend of action between rod and reel. The physical and mental connection between salmon and angler is felt most acutely in the rod hand. The vibrations coming up the line and through the rod into the hand and forearm are

Boyd Pfeiffer returns a salmon he has handtailed. Handling a fish this way is less taxing for the fish than is netting. Fewer scales are removed and the fish is not subject to excessive bruising.

instantly passed to the brain. The practiced hand automatically increases and decreases pressure as needed to maintain the steady application of tension. You feel the fish's every move and it feels yours when the contest is joined perfectly. For this reason, I am strongly in favor of a fly rod held in the right hand, if you favor it, and in the left if you're a port-sider. The rod should be in the sensitive or "smart" hand and the reeling done with the less schooled fingers. Switching the rod back and forth from one to the other for reeling purposes wastes time, and during the switch, a sudden movement of the fish may not be responded to quickly enough. There are times in boats, while wading, working along a brushy bank, and the like, when changing hands is necessary. But for better fish control, learn to use the "dumb" hand for reeling.

A good angler, in addition to having more fun while playing the fish, ends the battle as quickly as is practical. He's also a good sport, if the fish is to be released. A fish that isn't fought to absolute exhaustion stands a much better chance of survival. A salmon, or any species for that matter, that is played gingerly and kept on the hook much longer than necessary is not likely to survive. It's much better that they swim away after being unhooked with a wiggle in the tail rather than a listless off-center wobble. Salmon can be whipped with extremely light tackle and very small diameter leaders, but anything less than four pounds usually requires a much longer fighting period with the salmon being literally "fondled to death."

After unhooking, if the fish doesn't dart away, hold it by the "wrist" in front of the tail and support its midsection in a mild current and allow it to resume breathing steadily. If the gills are working sporadically, pump the fish gently by moving it back and forth, forcing more water into its mouth. You'll feel strength returning to its body, and within a minute or so it will wag off into the deep water. All but the most severely damaged or tired fish can survive, and most do if not nabbed by a natural predator soon after release. That's not likely to happen with the angler still close by.

The recuperative powers of Atlantic salmon are amazing. I've seen fish with net scars so deep that raw meat was showing go through spawning chores with gusto. I've caught grilse that fought with great fury and discovered at landing time that their entire dorsal fins had been ripped off in a gill net. I once caught a ten-pound fish that had suffered some sort of bite on the back of the head (from a seal perhaps) that was so deep the backbone was exposed—yet it had taken a fly and jumped several times during a fine battle. Fellow angler Bob Korosec once caught a salmon four miles upstream from where he'd lost the same fish the day before. He was sure, since his fly, a Black Bear Red-Butt, and twelve inches of leader tippet were still attached to the fish's jaw. The fish fell for the same pattern twenty-four hours later. A kamikaze salmon for sure!

9

*Which Fly Shall
I Try First?*

Drawing from experience and evaluating the type of food present and water condition of the moment, the trout fisherman can choose a fly from his box using logical deduction. The salmon angler can too draw from experience, but that's about the end of the streamside sleuthing. Because trout are almost always on the lookout for food, the decision of what to toss at them is a reasonable one. Salmon don't swallow food while on their romantic journey, so we must appeal to their curiosity, anger, or defense mechanisms. For a time British fly tying "pope" George Kelson and not a few of his disciples had the notion that salmon mistook the bright flies for butterflies, which they "remembered" from their youthful days as parr. Since butterflies are not common on all salmon rivers (and parr would have a tough time swallowing a butterfly anyway), this theory was soon put to rest. It did serve a purpose though: trying to duplicate the brilliance of butterflies created some strikingly beautiful fly patterns. And lo, the salmon actually rose up to grab them and some *were* fully as large as a big butterfly . . . and larger. That doesn't help the tyro, however, who is now gazing into his fly box with each little spring-clip holding a different combination of colors. And even if a fly is chosen with some confidence, what about size?

I think it can be safely stated that the greatest number of salmon flies cast at North American and Icelandic salmon are dressed on number 6 hooks of standard weight and shank length.

From maker to maker, hooks vary. Sometimes more than somewhat. One man's 6 becomes another's 8 or perhaps 4. The three most widely used salmon hooks today are the standard weights as made by Mustad, Partridge, and Tiemco. Without elaborating a great deal, I'll state that all three of these are acceptable salmon hooks of the black-enameled, up-turned eye style. The Mustads are the least expensive, are slightly larger than the other two size for size, and have the largest eyes. The Partridge is the most expensive, has the nicest-looking bend, and is made from extremely hard steel. The Japanese Tiemcos have the sharpest factory points I've ever seen, light steel (but plenty strong), and the smoothest enamel finishes. All will hold a salmon just fine, and if you tie your own, your choice will be determined by personal priorities.

Exactly why size 6 seems to work best on so many rivers is another wonderful salmon conundrum. On some rivers salmon feed on stoneflies, which are about a size 6, and a similar-size hook can lure the fish. But on rivers where there are no stoneflies, we search for another reason. Maybe many of the shrimp salmon eat in the ocean are of size 6. Whatever the reason, size 6 would certainly be my first choice on rivers of average size, say fifty to seventy-five yards wide. Don't worry about the salmon not seeing such a fly in rapid or deep water. Their ability to spot something on or near the surface is uncanny. Unless the guide or fellow angler who had fished the river previously suggested some local favorite, I'd probably tie on something with a black body, say, the Black Bear Green-Butt, Blue Charm, or Thunder and Lightning. This is mostly because I like black-bodied flies, and they've been good to me in the past. I'd fish them first with a straight knot for a while, allowing the fly to swing with the current in a natural way. If that produced nothing, I'd try the same pattern with a Portland hitch. If a fish showed but didn't take, I'd try the same cast a few more times and then rest him a few minutes. If the same cast didn't work, I'd go to a similar or identical pattern a size smaller. Work the drill again. If that didn't work, I'd try a larger fly of the same color scheme. If all this failed, I'd return to size 6 again and begin changing patterns. All this, mind you, only if I saw a fish. After thirty casts or so, I'd try another location if nothing had been spotted. Some anglers stick with a likely lie much longer, but I prefer to try another spot and maybe come back to the starting point at a later hour.

There is some truth to the old salmoneer's axiom, "Bright day, bright fly—dull day, dull fly." Bright days tend to cause a bright fly with a tinsel body or a flashy body wound with tinsel to catch and reflect the available light. There are some fish that are absolute pushovers for silver- or gold-bodied flies, in the sun or not. Perhaps this also has something to do with the food that particular fish enjoyed eating while in the salt water. If I were faced with a fish that came again and again to a darkish fly but wouldn't

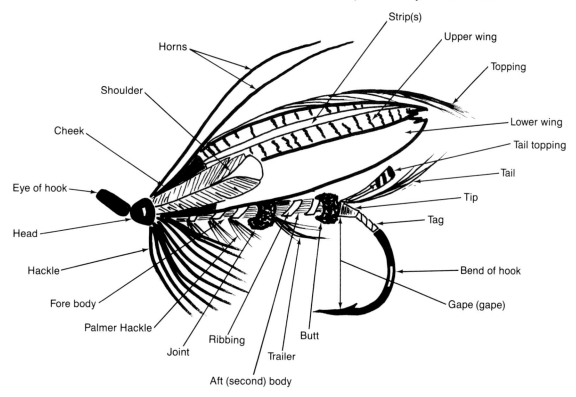

take, I'd certainly be tempted to switch to a silver-bodied fly. It may be mere coincidence, but it has always appeared to me that more of the ancient salmon patterns sported far more silver tinsel than gold. And then again, it may not have been coincidental at all. I've noticed that salmon seem to be more attracted to silver bodies than to gold, so maybe the old-timers knew what they were doing. This is curious in that several other anadromous species are much more attracted to gold, notably the shad and the herring. Tons of herring are caught each year in rivers on the Atlantic side of the U.S. on nothing more than a plain gold hook.

My absolute favorite silver-bodied fly is the sleek and sexy-looking Night Hawk. The feather wing version with its jet-black crow wing and silver body with red tag is a beautiful thing in the water. I feel it blends utilitarian black with the flashing silver in a nice way; greedily, I'm giving them black and silver in the same package.

The tried and true Silver Doctor is legendary as a "bright day" fly, and who can deny its beauty? Yet for all the lore behind it, I haven't caught many fish on the Silver Doc, but I've seen plenty of other anglers use it to good effect on well over a hundred

This bright salmon fell for a somber black fly. The day was overcast, proving the dark-day, dark-fly theory.

fish. (Hmmmm, maybe I should use it more often.) The Silver Rat, on the other hand, with no illustrious past as a classic pattern, was Canadian born and bred. A simple fly really, with nothing more than a tinsel body, squirrel tail wings, with a grizzly hackle wound around. A red head is optional (I kind of like it), but I've never been able to determine if the salmon care. But the Silver Rat in its basic dressing has got to be one of the magic flies of Canada. Many guides declare that if a fish will come to a silver fly on any day, it'll come to a Silver Rat. I agree.

Another fly I'd consider as a starting pattern, particularly in waters heavily stained with tannin (and many salmon rivers are), would be the previously mentioned Eldon Special. With its black body and barred red or fox squirrel wing, it has proven to be deadly on many occasions. And right about now is an excellent time to bring up a pet notion of mine that always comes to mind when discussing fly patterns. I call it the *staccato effect.*

Many tail hairs from an assortment of mammal tails are shaded in such a way that dark bands are formed. In the case of some squirrel tails, it might be argued that the bands are light on dark instead of vice versa, but deciding which is better is up to the eye of the beholder. A different sort of mottled effect occurs with groundhog (woodchuck), gray fox, silver monkey, and a number of other tails and body hair. These are speckled masses of dots and dashes. The Eldon Special also wears a few throat sprays of teal duck, which are black and white barred. The Eldon Special is a fairly recent creation, as are most of the hairwing flies, but this staccato thing has been around a long time. Consider the materials that have been commonly used on salmon flies since the art of making them first surfaced in the eighteenth century. Golden, silver, and amherst pheasant neck feathers are strikingly barred with black. So is summer (wood) duck, and most of the other duck flank feathers. Jungle cock "eyes" are spectacularly barred, as is bustard, turkey, and guinea. By accident or design, the early creators of fancy salmon flies fiddled with feathers long into lamp-lighted nights to achieve their stylized patterns—a great number of which clearly show this dot-dash, or staccato, effect.

It amounts to a break-up of the overall color silhouette. If, as some pundits believe, fish cannot distinguish color, a fractured silhouette might prove to be interesting. Ribbing on a fly body adds to the effect, as does the black ostrich herl butt so common on classic patterns; so does any contrasting butt for that matter. Tails, hackles, cheeks, and midbands can also be added in ways that compound the stop-and-start profile. An outstanding modern example of this is the highly effective Colburn pattern, which is used to great effect on Maine rivers. The body is nothing more than fluorescent green floss broken in the center by a band of black chenille or ostrich herl. Take another look at some of the fly illustrations in this book, and you'll immediately see what I mean. An all-black or an all-any-color fly can and will catch salmon, but I honestly believe that one with the "staccato" built in will have a better chance.

Jack Wise hooked this sixteen-pound Atlantic at Camp Pool Two while fishing out of Clyde House's camp on the Hunt River in Labrador. The fish had porpoised there for two days before Jack coaxed it with a Black Bear Red-Butt.

Since the matter of fish distinguishing color was passed over quickly last paragraph, some additional comment seems fair. Nearly half a century of fishing for a variety of species has convinced me that fish do perceive color. That they "see" color as we do is suspect—and the fish will never tell us—but plenty of reliable tests have shown that they respond to color graduations. Pavlovian tests in laboratory aquariums have shown beyond much doubt that fish will eat red pellets at a programmed feeding time and will not touch the green ones (or was it vice versa?). Anyway, whatever those crazed scientists appeared to prove had already been proven a thousand times over by a dozen generations of wet fly fisherfolk since Dame Juliana Berners was tying flies on her bent needles.

When a fly is under the surface, or in the surface film, fish certainly do seem to show a preference for one color over another when the notion strikes them. Flies floating on the very tips of their hackles or legs are another matter. I've spent dozens of water-logged hours in swimming pools looking up at dry flies against sunny and dull skies and have yet to see more than the slightest suggestion of color. Flies tend to appear as gray or black silhouettes. But I still wouldn't declare adamantly that fish aren't able to select one shade over another. The general shape or silhouette is probably the deciding factor, but how can we know that a fish's eye can't define minute variations in shades of gray? Certain materials also reflect light in curious ways, such as seal fur and peacock herl. What the fish sees may not be colors as we identify them, but I'm convinced they are quite discerning when the mood strikes them.

10

Tradition Unbound

For nearly forty years, salmon anglers going to or coming from salmon fishing in the Canadian maritime provinces stopped at Wally Doak's tackle shop in Doaktown, New Brunswick. Doak had the right tackle, the best selection of flies, the most up-to-the-minute information about the Miramichi River, and world-class fishing conversation. My first visit to this important little shop occurred in 1959 when I had little salmon fishing experience. My head was full of advice – written and oral – and I had tied proven flies as instructed by J. Edson Leonard in his fine book, *Flies*.

For all my preparation, however, I was not prepared for the sight that greeted me in the showcase nearest the door. In this glass-topped treasure box were row after row of partitioned trays containing more salmon flies than I thought existed in the world. There were hundreds of dozens of beautifully tied little gems that needed no special lighting. They had a life of their own and no salmon angler, including those who tied flies themselves, could resist buying a few if for no other reason than to say later, "Yeah, I bought that fly at Wally Doak's." But as a rank beginner in those days, I had to ask the obvious question: "Do the salmon really care?"

Doak was a fine talker and was not above selling anyone a bit more tackle than would be needed, but he must have taken note of the stunned look on my face as he leaned across the counter and in a stage whisper answered, "No, but the fishermen do and that's what sells flies!"

With nearly thirty years of salmon fishing behind me, I'm still asking that same question, and so are other anglers. The species is not important. Trout, bass, muskie, and walleye fishermen, and those who ply the salt water, spend an equal amount of time pondering the fly and lure selection problem. Some brave souls solve the selection bugaboo by becoming one-lure, one-fly, or one-bait fishermen: They reach a point of such certainty that they fish for certain species with certain lures or flies almost exclusively. Other fishermen believe imitation to be the sincerest form of flattery – they tailor their tactics to certain waters, learning what works from those who fish a place most often. Members of both camps have much to recommend their points of view, but one factor common to both – the belief that what they use will work – can make both traditions unbounded successes.

The one-fly, one-lure, and one-bait anglers are nearly always good fishermen who know their waters well and fish them frequently, sometimes exclusively. Because they know their home stream, river, lake, or bay so intimately, they have learned where, when, and how to cast old reliable for best effect. You won't beat them on their own water except by paying attention to how they do it and then building on this knowledge.

No matter how clever you may be, the locals will wipe your eye very quickly. Even the best of professional tournament bass catchers admit that without a day or two of practice fishing on an unfamiliar lake, they'd have a tough time knowing where, how, and what to fish with. The pro will fish with any lure or device that isn't rejected under the rules, but – and this is most pertinent – some of them are a hairbreadth away from being one-lure anglers.

I have a group of friends I enjoy fishing with, and for the past ten years I've made it a practice to spend a week each July on the Gros Mecatina River in Quebec. We're usually there the third or fourth week of July, but in 1985 we selected the first week of July, in which the earlier fish are scarcer but usually larger. It was the wrong decision. An ice blockage in the Strait of Belle Isle postponed the salmon's arrival along the entire north shore and most Gaspé rivers. To put it bluntly, there were no salmon. Instead, we filled the week with a small measure of brook trout fishing, much grumbling, and an interesting project.

Dave Randall, our resident attorney among the Mecatina Irregulars, filled his time poring over ten years' worth of camp records and compiled nearly everything worth compiling. He listed numbers of fish caught, pools in which they were taken, average pounds of fish per pool, and other trivia. Of great importance to me, however, was his list of fly patterns that caught fish.

With a total of 2,815 salmon caught over the ten-year period studied, it would be expected that certain patterns would come to the top. Did they ever. The Eldon Special was the number-one fly, accounting for a total of 370 fish. In a close race for second place were the Silver Rat and the Black Bear (Green-Butt) with 214 and 213 salmon, respectively. The Rusty Rat was fourth with 179. The Bomber (Cigar-Butt) with 157 was fifth, and after that, traditional patterns such as Blue Charm, Butterfly, Cosseboom, Black Rat, and Jock Scott started showing up with lesser numbers. A host of common and special patterns accounted for a fish or two, but the predominance of the Eldon Special was a real eye-opener.

Eldon Bobbitt, the camp owner's brother and the chief guide on the Mecatina, is a superb salmon fisherman. He ties flies and probably knows more about where fish ought to be on a given day than anyone else who's fished the river. He sells flies to the guests, and as any good businessman knows, if you don't use your own product, it's difficult to convince others to try it. He fishes his Eldon Special almost exclusively, and he catches salmon on it with annoying regularity. Guests have incentive to try it. The fact is, more Mecatina River salmon have the opportunity to see more Eldon Specials float their way than any other pattern. Part of the reason for the Eldon Special's success is obviously the frequency of delivery. But there's a bit more to it than that.

The Eldon Special wears red squirrel wings, tied a bit on the sparse side. The hackle is black or reddish brown rooster, with a spray of barred teal at the throat. The body is black wool or floss (whichever is available). There is no rib, but there is a tip of yellow floss (or wool). Some Eldon Specials are varied with the tip being green, and some have yellow and green. The reason for the variations has more to do with availability of materials than with Eldon Bobbitt's desire to confuse fly tiers. In Eldon's opinion (and mine), the black body, the red squirrel wing, and the tad of teal at the throat are the important ingredients. Black-bodied flies are indeed the most consistent producers on all Quebec salmon rivers, and certainly they do well on salmon rivers the world over.

The fantastically beautiful salmon flies that grace the pages of angling books and wall-mounted cases in anglers' dens have caught and will continue to catch salmon wherever they're cast. But it's a universal truth that the more recent hairwing patterns have proven to be as effective—perhaps more so. They're also easier to tie and require less expensive materials. I'd guess, based on the Mecatina River Fly Survey and observations made on at least three dozen other rivers, that seventy-five percent of the Atlantic salmon caught in North America are taken on hairwing flies. And further, a good fifty percent of these flies sport black bodies. That's because hairwing flies with black bodies are attractive to the fish. Moreover, because of the flies' track records, fishermen believe they'll work, and that may be most important.

The practical salmon angler (if there can be such a creature!) might conclude from the foregoing paragraph that if a modest selection of flies wearing black bodies is carried from place to place, victory will be assured. For one angler it might, but for most of us it won't. Basic black will catch salmon all right and plenty of them, but there are times when they don't work and just as many times when any fly will do the job. And I mean that literally. Certain bright salmon will strike a bare hook or the most outlandish clump of feathers if it's cast to the right spot. When humans first began tying flies and discovered such fancy combinations of fur, feathers, and steel would catch salmon, they quickly learned that some creations worked better than others. Waxing eloquent about "their" flies spawned a new literary art form—angling journalism. No other outdoor pursuit has been more written about than fishing, and within that heading, flies and the fishing done with them for trout and salmon lead the pack for book title numbers. Within this proliferation of titles, ten thousand of them at least, the subject of flies themselves evokes more passion and discourse than any other. Some objectivity is possible here, and we try for it when we can, but we usually fail. Why certain flies catch fish, why they are tied as they are, why the person who created them applied a snippet of this and a bit of that is conversational food that sustains us for lengthy periods of no fishing. What glorious, harmless fun!

And Back to Tradition Again

Only the most unemotional and artless clod could hold a full-dressed traditional salmon fly between thumb and forefinger and not be charmed by its symmetrical beauty. The flowing feathers of the wing, the overlaying of body parts, and the deadly gleam of the enameled black hook, sharp as a serpent's tooth, blend into a whole that is beautiful to the eye and sensual to the touch. Creating such masterpieces is the pinnacle of the fly tier's art. Flies designed and tied for other species are lovely to look at too, such as the long streamers developed for New England landlocked salmon and the delicate drys cast over trout in many lands. But it's the traditional salmon fly with jungle cock eyes, shoulders of blue chatterer, flanks of wood duck, and strips of macaw, bustard, and swan that demand more attention. They are the precious gems of fly fishing and, like rare stones, worth having around merely for their own sake. While we don't *need* them, the same can be said for paintings by Rembrandt, cars from Maserati, or music by Beethoven. The world would simply be a less pleasant place without them.

As with all of the arts, the individual doing the work will eventually develop a style that becomes identifiable. A few bars of Brahms or Benny Goodman, and you know who it is. A quick peek at a portion of a painting by Salvadore Dali or Frederic Remington, and you know which is which. The accomplished tier of classic salmon flies imparts his or her imprint as well, and certain "schools" of fly tying technique have evolved. And again, just as with painting and music, debates continue about who was there first with the most influence.

With traditional salmon flies, the two brightest stars of the past hundred years are undoubtedly George M. Kelson and Thomas Edwin Pryce-Tannatt. Both Englishmen, Kelson and Tannatt achieved a level of fly tying skill that demands our attention and awe. Drawings of Kelson's flies and photographs of Tannatt's prove that they were masters of the art, but hold onto your hats–they did all of their fly tying *without a vise.* They held the hook between thumb and forefinger while attaching every shard of material that would form their wondrous creations!

A handful of tiers still disdain the vise (Lee Wulff is one of them), and many of today's best who use a vise can tie a respectable fly without one. I've tried making a salmon fly without a vise by following Kelson's directions, and I can assure you it's not unlike trying to dress yourself while wearing boxing gloves. It can be done, but it takes time. A practiced eye can spot a fly tied in the fingers, particularly a full-dressed salmon fly, among a box full of vise-tied flies. They have a tight, yet slightly informal look about them that gives an impression that the feathers have been handled a lot. Not scruffy, mind you, but displaying a kind of studied casualness. Vise-tied flies, done by someone who knows his business, can have this hand-tied look but are usually seen to be far more well executed when one side of the fly is compared to the other. A mirror image is what the tier is striving for. That the hand-tiers did so well at this is a marvel to me.

Any serious student of salmon flies should have Kelson's 1895 tome, *The Salmon Fly,* and Pryce-Tannatt's *How to Dress Salmon Flies* (1914). They form the "old testament" of salmon fly tying, or "dressing" as the British choose to call it. A first printing of either is difficult to find and will set one back the price of a decent fly rod, but later editions are available from Angler's and Shooter's Bookshelf, Goshen, Connecticut 06756. The facsimile edition of Kelson, published by the original company, is a nearly perfect duplicate in most ways and, in fact, better in some in that it's printed on acid-free paper. With these two books, and in bits of other British books, anglers who also tied flies did the best they could for at least a generation. The old *Herter's Fly Tying Manual* helped somewhat, but there was a serious problem here and abroad. With few exceptions, professional fly tiers weren't keen about revealing all of the secrets of fly tying. Illustrations and printed material can be helpful, but nothing in this world beats spending some time at the elbow of one who knows how to tie well.

As interest in fly fishing grew, more professionals began to share their tricks and knacks after World War II. In 1950 came J. Edson Leonard's landmark book titled *Flies.* I had been winding my own feathers and fur for ten years when I first laid hands on this treasure. For the first time in my life I actually understood how certain procedures ought to be done. The chapter on salmon flies, albeit short, remains a textbook example in how to intelligently illustrate fly tying via pen-and-ink drawings. A number of other worthwhile fly tying books came on the market during the seventies, but few of them shed much light on how to make salmon flies. Some of them were excellent basic how-tos, and some were slavish copies of what had come before.

Then, in 1977, we saw Eric Leiser's *The Complete Book of Fly Tying*. I'm usually turned off by titles that use the word "complete," because there isn't any such animal. But Eric's book was special. With drawings by Dave Whitlock, an outstanding fly tier himself, the intelligent placement of drawings with the appropriate text, and materials list, this book was exactly what the art needed. Helen Shaw's offering, bearing the straightforward title *Tying Flies*, came to us in 1979 and accomplished in photographs what Leiser's did with drawings. Both are excellent basic instruction guides but with little about salmon flies specifically. Leiser's book does contain a section on the salmon fly, and what's there is great. But all of us were still looking for the New Testament.

It arrived, as did so many fishing and fly tying books, in the late seventies (1978 to be exact), in the form of Poul Jorgensen's *Salmon Flies*, from Stackpole Books with introduction by Joseph D. Bates, Jr., who also knows a thing or two about the subject. Here in Jorgensen's book were not only easy-to-follow instructions for making the traditionals but the recipes for the other classic styles: the Dee strip-wings, the grubs, the hornets, and the modern hairwings. Wonder of wonders, the inside dope on how to make the General Practitioner was here too. I had pondered over this pattern for more than thirty-five years, trying to figure out how in hell it was put together. Every old British fly catalog had a color plate that included the G. Practitioner and an accompanying story about how effective it was. It certainly is a pretty thing—but they never told us how to make it. Jorgensen to the rescue!

In addition to a heap of strong how-to photos, the book included accompanying text that was well thought out and complete. There were no abbreviated messages such as "now, tie on the tail." Jorgensen took the reader by the hand and walked him through each operation. And still of more value to today's maker of salmon flies, the book lists substitute feathers and ways to dye those that need it to duplicate some of the old materials. I mean, who has ever seen an Indian Crow or a Cock-of-the-Rock?

Hot on the heels of Jorgensen came Keith Fulsher and Charles Krom with *Hair-Wing Atlantic Salmon Flies*. Published by *Fly Tyer* magazine (North Conway, New Hampshire), this 180-page paperback is chock full of how-to fly tying and salmon fishing dope revolving around the use of today's favorite hairwing flies. The tying instructions are excellent, and so are the color plates. It's also obvious that Fulsher and Krom have stuck the iron into more than a few Atlantic salmon. For my money, these last books mentioned are the "new testament" of Atlantic salmon fly tying. There will no doubt be some others that will come on the scene one day, and I've probably overlooked other modern fly tying writers' books. My only defense is, I haven't read them all!

Since the books mentioned handle the subject of fly tying so well, I won't attempt to reinvent the wheel. As we move on in this discussion of flies, I'll mention certain ways of tying some patterns and special materials I've found to be useful, but mostly I'll be dealing with specific patterns and when they seem to work best. But we should clear up a fuzzy area that seems to confound anglers, writers who fish, and those other folks in the equally fuzzy world of critics.

My definition of critics is that they are those people who belong to the "they" group. You know, "they" say that . . . so on and so on. Some of these "they" people say that fly tying is not an art, it's a craft. According to "them" (closely allied with "they"), woodcarving is not an art either. Nor is making paper airplanes or fashioning a functional tool out of hot steel with anvil and hammer. If you've ever been to a duck decoy competition, watched a Japanese origami expert fold paper or a horny-handed blacksmith twist white-hot steel into a swinging gate, you know better. Yes, anyone with reasonable dexterity can tie a fly. The same can be said for painting with oils or fashioning a human likeness from a gob of clay. As in all such endeavors, few practitioners will reach the peak or close to it. The "average" fly tiers are merely that–as are those "average" folks who paint. But an artist is easily recognizable; the great fly tiers are artists. There, that's that.

I'm continually amazed at the recent surge of interest in traditional salmon flies and the new hairwing creations shown four times a year in *The American Fly Tyer* magazine. Some of these highly talented tiers are accomplished salmon anglers, but some have never seen a salmon river or the fish. Yet they are working earnestly at the fly tying bench trying to perfect their skills. A few are professional tiers; that is, they are commercial sellers of flies either through their own shops or other outlets. But most of them are spare-time tiers who tie simply because they like it. The salmon fly as a collector item has reached new status, and flies from some of the acclaimed experts such as Poul Jorgensen, Larry Borders, Alf Walker, and Scotland's Megan Boyd are seldom fished with. They reside in display cases and under the glass tops of coffee tables. And so they should, for they are works of art. Like artists in any medium, the top performers all have identifiable styles.

Having spent more than a little time at the fly tying bench over the past forty years, I have no illusions about my level of proficiency. My dry flies compare favorably with the run-of-the-mine tiers and so do the wets, streamers, and hairwing salmon patterns. My classic salmon fly efforts, however, need some refinement. Just when I think I've done rather well on a Durham Ranger or Jock Scott, I make the tragic mistake of laying my creation next to one tied by my friend Bob Ent, of Bangor, Maine. It's like comparing a pickup truck to a Rolls Royce. They'll both move down the road on four wheels, but they sure aren't the same. My flies will catch fish and they suit me just fine, but we're talking about masterful handling of feathers, fur, tinsel, and thread, resulting in a finished product that stands apart from lesser flies with total distinction. "Many are called but few are chosen!"

The color illustration on page 97 shows some examples of Bob Ent's artistry. In a project done specially for this book, Ent has tied a half dozen classics that have achieved international reputation. With the exception of the Silver Doctor, these half dozen patterns—Green Highlander, Dusty Miller, Blue Charm, Jock Scott, Thunder and Lightning, and Durham Ranger—are probably the best-known traditional patterns in the world. They have caught fish wherever Atlantic salmon are found. I asked Ent to proceed for two additional steps and tie the hairwing versions of all six and the reduced hairwing styles that are cast more often today. Studying these eighteen flies will reveal more about what the three types of flies look like than I could explain in several thousand words. They will also serve as models for those who would like to make classic flies.

Bob Ent freely admits that his fly tying hero was Pryce-Tannatt, and when possible he clings to that expert's patterns. Ent's style has indeed become highly personal. His flies are a bit more graceful than some in that they are sparser of wing and somewhat thinner in body. I hasten to point out this does not mean one style is right or another is wrong. They're just not the same. As the eye moves from classic to hairwings, it will be noted that while the materials become fewer in number, the overall color combinations and general hue of the flies remain the same. Some variations will also be spotted, such as the tip on the reduced hairwing Thunder and Lightning, which is red instead of yellow. When asked about this, Ent replied, "I like to tie it that way." And that's the way it is. To declare that any pattern must be tied just so is dogma of the worst kind. Even the old masters changed materials here and there, but the basic feathers used in the time-honored patterns remain the same—or at least the colors do.

While I freely admit that I am partial to Bob Ent's flowing style, with wing and tail meeting at a line parallel with the bend of the hook, I had to ask him which contemporary tiers he most admired. In addition to the previously mentioned names, Ent also included Ron Alcott, Bill Hunter, and Maxwell MacPherson. They are all New Englanders, which is not unusual considering that's where the salmon of the U.S. happen to be. The tradition of tying salmon flies is strong there and will probably continue to be. Classic flies from all of these tiers are of collectible quality, and prices range from twenty-dollars to more than thirty-five, depending on size and complexity of patterns. That's for a single fly. They're worth it!

Of particular interest to those who collect fancy flies or those who want to fish with the top-quality flies is the little catalog from Maxwell MacPherson, Jr. Eighty flies, mostly traditional patterns, are shown in full color on nice glossy paper. Max's prices range from $3.25 each for hairwings to $60 for a size 8/0 classic complete with gut-eyed hook. MacPherson will tie nearly any pattern on special order, but he specializes in duplicating old Kelson and Pryce-Tannatt styles, and several examples of both are also illustrated in his catalog. The address is 10 Hillside, Bristol, New Hampshire 03222.

Some hairwing patterns may deserve the term "classic" by this time. Certainly the Cosseboom, Hairy Mary, and Rusty Rat have been fished enough by plenty of anglers to prove their worth. But the "classic" label in salmon fisher parlance still means those patterns that have been around for a century or more, tied with feather wings and as close to the "original" as possible. Classic patterns can be tied on modern hooks, but to the true believer, an honest classic must still be tied on a straight shank hook with an eye of twisted gut. Practically all salmon flies were tied this way until the 1920s, and even today several British fly tackle houses still offer selections tied with gut eyes.

The transition from gut eyed to steel-eyed hooks was not accomplished overnight. Steel-eyed hooks were available in Pryce-Tannatt's day (1914), but he stated frankly that he didn't like them. Nor did the majority of other British salmon fishers and fly tiers. It was their strong belief that the flexible gut eye formed a smoother transition between leader and fly and allowed it to "turn freely" in the fish's jaw, resulting in a better hold. Nicely finished loop eyes, an extension of the hook itself, were offered by several hook makers shortly after Pryce-Tannatt's book appeared, and the gradual switch began. It's arguable if the gut eye made much of a difference, but there are anglers alive today who still insist on tying flies the old-fashioned way. Those who tie classics for sale or show will make them either way.

In addition to the hook used, a classic should feature a nicely tapered head, not too small and not too large. The feathers should be clean and bright, and the wing and crest should meet in such a way that the full profile of the fly forms a symmetrical oval shape. The black bars of a Ranger-type wing, formed by overlapping golden pheasant tippets, should be in line with each other. The final black bar should also coincide precisely with the black butt on the body. Five spiral ribs of tinsel on the body are considered proper, and the jungle cock eye should fall at the halfway mark on the body. And on it goes until the novice will begin to wonder if he can ever make the grade. Some of the rules for tying classics are listed in the old tomes previously mentioned; some are not. The best advice that can be offered to those who care is to study as many flies and illustrations of classics you can lay your hands on and try to emulate the ones that suit your fancy. Of course, try to spend some time watching a good tier at work. No surgeon ever learned how to perform an appendectomy through verbal instructions alone.

11

Flies: Beyond Black and Silver

One might assume from the foregoing chapter that the simplified approach of choosing either a basically black fly or one with a silver body will solve seventy-five percent of Atlantic salmon angling situations. In practice, this approach has done so for me and for a large number of other anglers. But casting at these wonderful fish is not a simple-minded pursuit because the other twenty-five percent of the time, when black or silver won't produce, seems to be the percentage we find ourselves in more often than not. Those times are when the fly pattern enigma begins to loom large. Traditional European fly tiers were constantly trying to outdo each other by creating complex combinations of colors and textures attached to hooks, but there just may have been some method to their madness. The snippet of blue, for example, as a shoulder, side feather, hackle, tail, or body, appears on so many traditional patterns that a more careful examination is called for.

Comparatively recent tests with sophisticated equipment have proven that the color blue is highly visible in deep or turbid water. Certain shades of green also stand out; red and orange do not. On or near the surface, red is easily discerned, but loses its brilliance quickly as it descends. As red goes deeper, it appears as black. Yellow, on the other hand, appears to become more whitish. (All this, of course, is as it appears to the human eye.) There can be little argument that fish are attracted to certain colors on certain days. Furthermore, all these factors are compounded by existing water clarity. The tournament bass anglers don't carry their assortment of lures just because they enjoy carrying a big tackle box.

I hear you: You're saying, "First we're told that a salmon will take nearly any fly and especially if it's black and silver, and now you're saying we've got to carry a much wider assortment for the problem days." Yes. Some other colors should be in the salmon fisher's well-rounded box, but every pocket filled to the brim with flies isn't required either. A couple sizes in ten or a dozen patterns will do the job. With that snippet of blue, for example, the choices are easy and overlap the black-and-silver combination in a highly complementary way.

This brings us to the Blue Charm, either the traditional version or the hairwing model. All of the good stuff is here. The body is black with silver rib; the wing (on the traditional) has the barring of mallard and teal; and the hackle is bright blue. It may be totally unprovable, but I'd guess that the Blue Charm, with its many minor variations, has been the undoing of more Atlantic salmon than any other fly in the world. A hairwing version of it requires nothing more than to substitute gray or fox squirrel tail hairs for the wing. It was not by whim that the first pattern chosen by Poul Jorgensen for a series of how-to photographs in his book *Salmon Flies* was a Blue Charm.

The Crossfield and the Silver Blue, nearly identical patterns, feature all-silver bodies, wings of barred teal, and blue hackle. A simple pattern indeed, but one to conjure with if a salmon-fishing trip to Iceland is on the itinerary. There is no doubt about it, Icelandic salmon show a decided preference for a touch of blue. They also like the Blue Charm and the Silver Doctor.

While the Silver Doctor is one of the best-known salmon patterns, I've always preferred the Blue Doctor. The Silver Doctor has a solid silver tinsel body with an oval silver ribbing and the Blue Doctor's body is of blue floss over-ribbed with oval silver tinsel. There isn't any objective reason for liking the blue body; it just appeals to me.

There are two other Doctor patterns—the Black Doctor and the Helmsdale Doctor. The Black Doctor is by far the better of the two in terms of ideal ingredients. It has the red butt, common with all of the Doctors, and a black body. The Helmsdale is nearly identical to the Silver model with the exception of yellow instead of blue hackle. I can never remember catching or seeing a salmon caught on a Helmsdale Doctor. Yellow hackle or other parts of the same shade work well on other patterns, but if there ever was a white elephant for me, it would have to be the Helmsdale Doctor. It's pretty, though.

The Doctor family, of which the four mentioned are the most prominent, does with the color red what other flies do with blue. There is just a tad of it at the butt and a similar bump at the head. The head bump used to be a clump of red wool or spun fur, but the fashion today is a stripe of red lacquer. Either style looks fine, but if used much, the red lacquer wears away during a day of hard fishing. As with blue or any other brilliant color, salmon seem to want it in measured doses. An all-blue or an all-red fly doesn't attract much attention . . . or at least it isn't the right kind of attention. With the exception of black, a fly wearing a solid coat of any color seldom finds many customers. Well, wait a minute, I did see several salmon caught one week on an *all-green* Muddler Minnow on the big George River up Ungava way. It was a terrible-looking fly that grew more terrible as the week passed. It was passed around from one angler to another, and, as I recall, six of us took fish on that same fly. It became a sort of "community" fly, and the original owner, an M.D. from Michigan, was charging a dollar a day to use it. Other flies took fish on that trip, but passing this fly around was fun.

To stick with green for a minute, and the George River as well, here is another place where a particular color can perform magic. The Cosseboom, the traditional Green Highlander, the old Grizzly King, and various hairwings sporting green or olive bodies perform extremely well on this water. If there were large stoneflies on the river with green bodies the explanation would be obvious. I won't say that there are no stoneflies on the George, but they're not plentiful. Other than the largest and hungriest black flies in the world, insects of any kind are not there in abundance. There just doesn't appear to be a reason for this, but in that blackish-green water (yes, it is green) flies with more than a dash of green rack up a better score than do most other flies. But black is good on the George too.

Since many of the old and new patterns, including some hairwings, call for a topping of golden pheasant crest, it might be assumed that this is a secret fish-getting ingredient. It might be just that. In the early days of salmon fly creation, the tiers who supplied their wares to the rich and royal were lavish in their use of color and texture. It seems certain they were trying to impress their customers with a multitude of feathers and complicated tying procedures. From a design standpoint, the artfully curved, golden pheasant crest feather is the perfect natural feather for the topping on an oval-shaped salmon fly. When the correct size is selected, the arching fibers of shiny gold meet the upturned tail (also golden pheasant) in a way that frames the other ingredients. Artistry aside, there is, I think, another reason for using golden pheasant. The feather barbules reflect light in a strange luminescent way.

The sparkle of golden pheasant crest feathers is common to few other birds. The Amherst pheasant has a red crest displaying the same odd sheen, and so have a handful of much rarer creatures. The herl, those greenish blue or bronze-blue barbules that grow from the long center quills of peacock tails, also have this strange glow. Among the mammals, polar bear hair actually seems to glow in the dark and sparkles under bright sun. Beaver, mink, and otter are less translucent than polar bear, but still reflect considerable light. Seal fur was also used by the old masters and is the shiniest fur I've ever seen. Some of the modern substitutes are quite good, but nothing beats real seal. All of these materials have been used on salmon flies at one time or another, and their worth has been well noted. Supplies of polar bear and seal are carefully guarded these days, but the other furs and feathers mentioned are not scarce.

I suppose the reason more peacock herl is not seen on many classic salmon flies or modern hairwings has more to do with durability than anything else. It is fragile and, unless a body of herl is reinforced with thread or fine wire, won't last long. Fish teeth, bushes, and water-soaking take their toll. But the loss of a few flies to wear and tear shouldn't deter anyone from using flies wearing peacock herl. The material is so effective, it shouldn't be overlooked. A common trout pattern, the Leadwing Coach-man, tied on a suitable hook has accounted for many salmon. The combination of peacock herl and white polar bear hair can also be applied to the universally known Royal Coachman. A mundane package to offer the princely salmon, I suppose, but it will work well at times.

By the time 1850 was seen on calendars, the salmon fishers of the British Isles and Ireland had more than a little angling experience stored in their minds and on paper. They were quite aware of the Atlantic salmon's moods and whims. While the British make much of doing things in a "sporting" manner, they were not above throwing spoons and hooks baited with prawns, earthworms, or whatever at the noble salmon if they wanted one for the table. I find it absolutely appalling that lure and bait fishing is still condoned there and in Iceland. Even on totally private water where fish are considered a cash crop, I strongly believe that Atlantic salmon should be taken on the fly or not taken at all.

A small measure of pontificating is useful here, because it leads us to three styles of salmon flies that I think came into being as a result of salmon eating live bait and flashing hardware.

On the rivers Dee and Spey in Scotland, flies tied to suggest something alive instead of the commonly used high-wing patterns were seen around the middle of the nine-teenth century. The Dee "strip" flies developed into a more or less long, skinny design with wings attached at the side of the hook shank instead of on top. The Spey flies evolved into a shorter fly tied on a standard length hook, usually sporting barred duck wings. Both styles were tied with extra-long hackle feathers taken from a blue heron or with saddle hackles from a large game fowl. The idea was to hackle the fly in such a way that the feathers appeared to have a life of their own, wriggling and undulating as the fly drifted or was pulled through the water. Neither style has ever gained many advo-cates on North American salmon rivers, but that's not to say they don't work. The late Vince Marinaro, of *A Modern Dry Fly Code* fame, had a minor love affair with Spey flies and used them to good effect on Nova Scotia's Margaree and Maine's Penobscot.

Tube flies are fashioned by tying a fly on a hollow cylinder made from plastic, hard rubber, or metal of the correct size and diameter. After the "fly" is tied, the end of the leader is passed through the tube and a treble hook attached to the loose end. These creations are effective but, in my opinion, come mighty close to being lures instead of flies. I've never used them and don't intend to. They have quite a following in Great Britain and Iceland. Since treble hooks are barred from most Canadian and U.S. Atlantic salmon rivers, it's doubtful we'll ever have occasion to use them.

A fourth style of fly, which is of great use to North American anglers, is the "low-water" variety. When the rivers drop in late summer and early fall, flies tied on standard salmon hooks may sink too fast to be of much use. The low-water ties are fashioned from steel about half the weight of, but slightly longer than, a standard hook. Any pattern can be tied as a low-water by attaching the tail at the halfway mark on the hook and finishing the fly at about half-size in relation to the hook. Such flies are usually tied sparsely and minus a few of the materials called for in a standard pattern. Low-water flies may also be tied on standard weight hooks if faster sinking rate is needed. The low-water fly gives the angler the hooking power of a larger hook while showing the fish a smaller fly.

All generalizations are dangerous when discussing flies and Atlantic salmon, but I'll stick my neck out with another one. The size and style (and colors too) of the fly we choose do indeed make a difference when we switch from one river to another. George Kelson, author of the nineteenth-century "bible" of salmon fly tying, carried this fly pattern discussion to the very heights of pompous pronouncement. He claimed he had devised a "system" for deciding which ingredients ought to be used in making flies for particular rivers at particular times. To Kelson, the difference between a single slip of blue macaw versus two of the same was monumental. So were a number of hackle fibers, precise length of tails, and so on. I have read Kelson's book *Salmon Flies* from cover to cover at least twice and have yet to determine what his "system" is. It appears

Low-water fly

that the system is whatever he wanted it to be at the moment. The book is, however, a beautiful thing and contains a wealth of useful fly tying and salmon fishing information. I'd give anything to have one of his flies. Well, almost anything!

Kelson nevertheless was not totally off base when he declared that certain patterns on certain rivers *can* make a big difference. So can size and style of fly. I don't think that salmon can count the number of tinsel stripes on a fly body or how many hairs there are in a hairwing, but a change of pattern, size, or color can trigger a reaction, causing a rise. I'm sure that the Portland Hitch can shake a fish out of the doldrums, and ditto with the Bomber. Big flies are usually associated with big rivers and small flies with small rivers, but here again, these are merely oft-told generalities. On some very small rivers, fish are caught with regularity on flies as large as 6/0 during a seige of high water. On the famous Moisie River on the north shore of the St. Lawrence, the reverse is true. The Moisie is certainly not a small river by most standards, yet the majority of fish taken there have risen to small flies. A size 6 is about as large as one should ordinarily use, with most fish being caught on 8s and 10s. And we're not talking about grilse here – the Moisie gives up salmon of more than thirty pounds every year.

I totally disagree with Kelson in the matter of educating fish from one generation to another. Old George believed that after a few seasons of seeing a particular pattern, the fish in that river actually remembered what it looked like, requiring the creation of a variation of the pattern to fool them. That a salmon can "remember" anything is doubtful; furthermore, remembering the differences between a Jock Scott and an Orange Parson from one year to the next is more than many anglers can do. A salmon simply doesn't have that many brain cells. While I've already mentioned that I don't believe that salmon act via some logical thought process but instead react, I must take a minor detour and allow that color and fly pattern are part of eliciting this reaction impulse.

Once, on the Sandhill River in Labrador, a guide remarked that the Thunder and Lightning hairwing was the best fly on the river except during the early morning hours; between sun-up and about 10:00 A.M. a Silver Rat or Silver Doctor would do better. As it turned out, the fish performed precisely as he said they would. The water was very low that day, but I did take one fish on an Echo Beach at about nine-thirty (the Echo Beach has a bright silver body) and two more fish in the afternoon on, of course, a Thunder and Lightning. I have no doubt that some other patterns might have done as well or better, but not all guides know their water so intimately. My pet theory about this silver-in-the-morning thing is that when the sun rises on the lower Sandhill pools, it stares the angler smack in the face and bounces off the water at a long, shallow angle. The side of the river most anglers fish from allows no shadow to cross the pool. But the sun's rays do strike a bright fly with intensity, probably causing a brilliant sparkle easily seen by the fish. Later in the day when the sun has passed beyond the angler and the fish are not somewhat blinded by it, darker flies are called for. They will show up better in subdued light.

On a number of salmon rivers there are pools that are known as good "morning" pools and some that traditionally produce better during the afternoon and evening hours. I'm sure that the angle of the sun's rays has a great deal to do with it. The Snakepit Pool on the Mecatina is a morning pool, no question about it. But curiously, it's better before the sun hits at full force. The pool is situated in a rocky chute, and most of the water is shaded until nearly 10:00 A.M. Until that hour comes, a morning can see fish after fish rise to the fly with abandon. Things slow down over the next hour, and by high noon it might be all over for another day. It is, if the day is bright and sunny. If the sky remains gray and overcast or if rain falls, the action can continue. Discussing this with other anglers and guides has verified the existence of morning and afternoon pools.

I'll carry this sunlight angle a step further. The way the sun strikes a pool varies little from day to day, but over a season will shift several degrees. We know, of course, that there are few hours of daylight in the northern hemisphere as autumn approaches. As the days dwindle down and September arrives, the angle of the sun's rays becomes less acute. Without getting into a highly scientific can of worms (or box of flies), I'll state simply that the way a salmon sees a fly is altered as well. The fish may see more or less of the complete profile, or because of new shadows and water levels be less or more inclined to rise. Hence, some pools produce better in July than they do in September. Water height and a comfortable position on the part of the salmon are undoubtedly factors, but the angle of the light source could be the most important reason the fish respond. As with so many puzzles in the game of fishing for Atlantic salmon, we'll never know for sure.

Having tied flies since age nine, and never losing my love affair with them, I find it difficult to stop rambling on about them. While it's been written many times that the expert fly fisherman can, with one pattern, catch trout and salmon around the world; stated another way, the angler armed with a vest full of flies and no skill might not catch any. It would be a terribly tedious game if every Atlantic salmon chose to eat a Jock Scott or Cosseboom to the exclusion of all other patterns. The fisherman would soon tire of the sport, and the bored fly tiers would all be in mental institutions. Creating new patterns and variations of old ones is what keeps a fly tier at the vise long into the night. It doesn't matter that seventy-five percent of our "new" flies don't work any better than the old favorites. Hope that they will keeps us playing with our feathers.

In the case of trout, the one-fly angler can do extremely well, but there will be times when he'll wish he had a different fly or two. The salmon angler with one pattern in his box is handicapping himself in the extreme. Since it is my contention that the salmon itself has little idea of what it's rising for, how in the world can the angler know?

More than one angler has tossed a cigarette butt, a twig, a flower blossom, or whatnot into a salmon pool after failing to get a rise, only to see a fish boil up and grab the hookless object. Does that tell us that we should make flies that look like twigs, cigarette butts, and flowers? Well, Bombers do look a lot like sticks or butts, and some of the fancy flies we throw at the fish resemble flowers. The chances are, if a fly instead had drifted over the fish with the strange preference it more than likely would have taken the fly. It was *ready* to take, and whatever drifted over it did so in an interesting way.

Fish don't resemble humans in many ways. It would be wonderful if they could talk, but then if they could, we probably wouldn't be challenged to fish for them. The taking of our fly into their mouths is done because fish don't have any fingers. If they want to examine, destroy, or eat anything, they've got to take it into their mouths. Regardless of the motive – hunger, fear, competitiveness, anger, or mere curiosity – they must hold an object in their mouths in order to make some distinction. I submit that all of these motives come into play at some time or another in a salmon's reactionary mind. They may not digest food while on their way to the spawning redds, but they do take in insects. They show fear by bolting away at the touch of the hook. A school of salmon can be highly competitive with the quickest off the mark being the one you'll hook on certain days. They can show anger by fighting with other fish for the right to fertilize newly dropped spawn. And few who've seen a salmon play with a fly for half a dozen casts can doubt that these fish are highly curious when they choose to be. For all of these reasons I carry more flies along salmon rivers than I should, and many of them will never get wet. But I want them with me . . . just in case!

For the beginner to select from, and the experienced angler to compare, here is a basic list of wet and dry flies that should cover most Atlantic salmon situations. Sizes are not specified, but for most North American rivers, size 6 will be the most useful. Before embarking on any salmon adventure, ask the lodge owner, booking agent, or someone who's been there before which sizes are most frequently used.

Silver-bodied Flies

Silver Rat
Silver Doctor
Night Hawk
Silver Wilkinson
Mar Lodge
Note: All of these can be tied in hairwing style or traditionally with feathered wings. The only one I'd insist on being traditional would be the Mar Lodge.

Black Flies

Black Bear Green-Butt
Black Bear Red-Butt (or Conrad)
Black Doctor
Black Dose
Black Woodchuck (a Black Bear Green-Butt with woodchuck tail for wings)
Note: There are many hairwing and traditional patterns wearing black bodies. All of them can be useful—whatever suits your fancy.

Blue Flies

Blue Charm
Crossfield (good silver pattern as well)
Blue Doctor
Benchill
Silver Doctor (blue hackle, thus qualifying for blue and silver)
Blue Rat

Gray Flies

Silver Gray
Gray Rat
Grizzly King (qualifies as a green fly too)

Green Flies

Green Highlander (traditional and hairwing)
Cosseboom
Green Rat
Green Woodchuck (Grizzly King tied with woodchuck wings)

Other basic colors are covered nicely with several traditionals and the hairwing versions, such as:
Dusty Miller (a little bit of everything)
Jock Scott (black and yellow)
Thunder and Lightning (black and orange)
Durham Ranger (black, blue, and orange)
All of the "Rat" series—Rusty Rat, Black Rat, and the others—are included under specific colors. Note: While the absolute finest wing on any rat is silver monkey, it's

almost impossible to obtain. Guard hairs from the neck of the gray fox are the perfect substitute.

Of course some Bombers must be included. As a starter, acquire some on long-shank (3X) hooks with a wide gape. Sizes 2, 4, and 6 will cover most situations. Deer body hair works well, but caribou floats better. A bleached white Bomber will be useful at times, but the best color is natural tan wound with a white or reddish brown rooster hackle.

A selection of standard dry flies should include:

The Wulff series of dry flies (Royal, Gray, and White)
Brown, black, and gray Bivisibles (just a lot of hackle wound on to fill the hook)
Curt Hill's Haystack (my current favorite)
Elk Hair Caddis (or something similar with a down-wing)
Black, brown, and white spiders (tied with extra-long saddle hackles and tails)
The Adams (yep, this old favorite trout fly tied on a stout size 10 or 8 hook is a dandy)
The Wilson Dry Fly Hook is the one to use for most dry flies. It is extremely light, and the points and barbs are nicely made. Size 10 will be most useful with 8s, and 12s a tie for second place.

Double Hooks: Boon or Handicap?

Within each general group of flies mentioned, excepting the drys of course, a couple of double-hook flies ought to be included. On some rivers where the Atlantic salmon is king, the use of double hooks is the standard approach. On other rivers, the heavier doubles, of any size, are seldom considered. As with all matters concerning the Atlantic salmon, there is no cut-and-dried answer. Well, there is for some anglers who absolutely won't fish them and for others who use them to the exclusion of anything else. I choose a middle-ground position that is probably as rigid as the extreme points of view.

There are times when salmon prefer an extremely small fly. A single size 10 or 12 will hook and hold a big fish all the way to net or beach, but a double hook of the same size will do it better. When fish want the fly a little deeper, the double hook will sink quicker and drift through the productive water at a slower rate. Such a drift is needed in some pools during high-water periods. Likewise on the large rivers with heavy current, a double hook is valuable if for no other reason than to get the fish's attention. But double hooks, for all their deadly good looks, with two wicked points instead of one, can be counterproductive much of the time.

One of the most popular notions held by double-hook fanciers is that the twin barbs serve as outriggers to keep the fly upright as it glides past a salmon's nose, thus allowing the fish to see the entire profile. Maybe, but with a single hook floating flat on the surface or just beneath, the entire profile can be seen even more sharply. A minor consideration. The double-hook buffs counter with: Two hooks are better than one during a long fight with a big fish. To this I respond: True, but only with double hooks up to size 4. Beyond that point, it has always appeared to me that one hook seems to act as a lever against the other, and soon two holes are torn in the jaw that eventually meet—probably causing a lost fish at the moment of truth.

I'm also convinced that many salmon have risen to seize a double-hook fly, but at the second the jaw begins to close, a fish feels the unyielding steel and backs away or shakes it loose. With the smaller doubles, those below size 4, this is less likely, and the tiny barbs bite with a vengeance. If only one hook sticks a salmon at the hinge of the jaw and the other barb is outside the jaw, the leverage against the hook doing the holding can quickly dislodge it—usually on the first jump.

I regularly carry some doubles in the small sizes but never any larger than size 4. Some years ago I fished a lot with doubles much larger than that, and while I hooked a fair number of fish with them, I didn't land nearly as many as was the case with single hooks. I really believe that a fish taking a single hook in its mouth stands a much better chance of being hooked. The single hook will roll and adjust in the fish's mouth and twist to encounter bone or flesh as the fish moves away—by the time you feel the "pull," the fish is hooked. I've felt many strong pulls on a double hook and nothing after that. The fish felt the nearly forty-five-degree angle between the twin hooks and didn't clamp down. The bottom line? Carry a few small doubles and some big ones if you must, but be prepared to lose some fish.

Eventually, every tier of salmon flies will gravitate to a style of his or her own. If you do make your own, vary the heft of the dressings from time to time so you have some thick ones as well as some that are thinly dressed. This simply involves using less wing, less hackle and applying a thinner body if you are inclined to dress your flies heavily. The reverse if you're a graceful tier. The general rule is lightly dressed flies in low water and chunky flies in fast or deep water—but remember too about that awful generality trap!

12

The Dry Fly and the Salmon

The act of a salmon rising purposefully to snatch a dry fly from the surface is the part of this study that evokes the most heated conversations. I'd like to turn up the thermostat another degree or two by suggesting that any salmon, if given the right opportunity, will rise to a floating fly. Pretty dogmatic, huh?

It will surely be noted by a number of salmon chasers that I allowed myself an escape hatch by inserting the words "right opportunity." On some waters, and in some specific pools, that right opportunity seldom if ever presents itself, but more often than not it will. For the traveling angler in search of Atlantic salmon not to carry some floating flies in his vest is a mistake . . . yet a heap of us continue to rely on wet flies only.

There are rivers frequented by Atlantic salmon where the use of the dry fly has become more or less standard procedure. Well, it's standard for those who have dry flies with them and have some idea how to use them. The Hunt River in Labrador is an excellent example, and so is the Eagle in the same province. Most of the New Brunswick rivers offer good dry fly opportunities in certain pools and at correct water levels. Now these provisions aren't disclaimers, they're simply facts. After all, dry flies are not precisely the right things to use on a brown trout stream at *all* times of the year.

In most parts of the British Isles and in Ireland, the local talent will usually be found defending the "across and downstream drift," and occasionally the "dead" drift, which involves mending the line regularly as the wet fly coasts along just beneath the surface. Until quite recently, Icelandic guides and pedestrian anglers felt the same way about salmon-coaxing on that island. And even on some large salmon rivers on the "enlightened" continent of North America, it's been the slinging of sunken hooks that's accounted for most fish. The popular notion has long been that a salmon, particularly a large one, is not keen about poking its nose out of water to seize a bunch of floating feathers or hair. Hmmmmmm. It has long been a minor wonder to me why some otherwise thoughtful salmon anglers can't accept the idea that if a salmon can see and is attracted to a fly just at or barely beneath the surface, it will also come to a fly on the surface. Well, it will if the prevailing conditions permit it to.

On a large and awesome river such as the Grand Cascapedia or, say, the fearsome George in the Ungava Bay region, a dry fly is likely to be ignored by most fish in the typical runs. This is not because the fish won't take them, but rather because seldom does a fish have the chance to rise from the depths and meet the fly in an ideal way. Low water or placid water is not a common scene on these rivers, and to get the fish's attention in the first place, the fly has to be quite heavy and "held" in the productive water long enough to be seen. A size 4 or larger single or double hook will be more productive here, because the fish has a chance to get it before it's swept away. But . . . fish of the George can be taken on dry flies if a spot is located where fish will lie in current that permits the floating fly to be drifted properly. There is a beautiful long run on the east bank of the George almost directly opposite Conluci Snowball's camp, which is some twelve miles up from salt water. The main flow is split by a covey of large boulders, and to the east the rippling current enters a long run with considerably less force than is the case along the west shore. This stretch of gently rolling water is about six feet deep with a bottom of baseball-size rocks. From across the river, the area doesn't look like a salmon lie, because it appears to be nearly dead water. But it isn't, and the flow is just right for the drifting of a dry fly or a riffle-hitched wet. The length of this flow is about three hundred yards and at the tail end of it is a popular spot for the four- to five-pound char that almost pollute this part of the river.

During an adventure on the George in 1978, with the then-editor of *Field & Stream*, Jack Samson, we worked this spot one morning. The mission was to catch char for picture purposes, and we had no trouble doing it. The hard-fighting char would grab a bright orange or red streamer on almost every cast, and (I apologize for saying it) it didn't take long to tire of the sameness of these fish. Lots of fun for a fish or six, but after that it was old hat. Every fish was a clone of the previous one. As I squinted through the camera lens recording Jack releasing one, I saw a much larger "hump" in the water at the head end of the run. It was either a big char or an Atlantic salmon. Our guide assured us that what I'd seen wasn't a salmon, since no salmon had ever been caught on this side of the pool. Of course that's all the encouragement crazy Yankees need to cast themselves into exhaustion. We eased up the river to the top of the pool and climbed out of the double-ended *bateau*. The rocks were a bit tough to walk on, but we could wade to a comfortable casting distance from where I'd seen the fish roll.

Jack was into a fifteen-pound fish within half a dozen casts. It took a size 2 Black Dose, and he beached it in short order. Ten feet from the spot he hooked his fish I was into one nearly as soon. It took a size 4 Muddler. But the neat thing was, it had grabbed that Muddler as it was drifting along on the surface. Actually, I hadn't planned it this way, the fly simply floated as if it had a mind to. A happy accident! Since I love to catch fish on the surface when possible, I went the extra mile and laid some dry fly floatant onto the now-proven Muddler. This time, on purpose, I cast the fly upstream and allowed it to drift through the pool in a typical "dead" fashion. Just as the fly reached its maximum drag-free position, there was a beautiful boil behind it and a tail appeared that looked as wide as a snow shovel!

The next cast had him but the hook didn't get a good grip, and with one headshaking leap the fish continued its journey to wherever it was going. To shorten the tale of our fishing prowess to a few lines, let it be noted that we scarcely left this pool for four days. There was no need to. New salmon moved in each evening, and we'd raise a fish on nearly every trip down the run. We took turns wading the length of it, trying not to hammer any non-taking fish too much. We caught several salmon each and rose and lost fully as many. While the fish would come to wets and drys, they actually preferred the floating flies. On many occasions we'd have them show for the wet and then take the dry. It should be observed here that on most salmon rivers exactly the reverse seems to be the experience of well-traveled anglers.

As with dry-flying over sophisticated brown trout, the ideal water for the salmon dry fly is not a run where twisting and conflicting currents cause a floater to drag crazily. A smooth, steady flow is what we want, where the fly drifts at a consistent speed and the salmon has the chance to see that its travels are not being held up by unseen forces. Oh, to be sure, a dragged fly and even one that makes a wake across the surface will catch many a salmon, but for those positive rises the dead drift will outfish the worked or jiggled fly most of the time, the reason being that the deliberate take of a smoothly floating fly is far more likely to result in a solidly hooked fish. And here we have arrived at the heart of the dry fly problem for many anglers. Salmon don't grab a fly in the same way a trout does; and the angler must *really watch* that fly to do well at the moment of truth.

I have heard many guides and many salmon chasers expound on when and how to strike salmon that come to a floating fly. Some of the advice is good and some isn't, but even the "blind hog finds an acorn once in a while," as the saying goes. Some fish have kamikaze genes and will get themselves hooked no matter what the angler does. But they are not in the majority, and to hook Atlantic salmon with some consistency on dry flies requires the fishermen to remain frozen until that fly *actually disappears into a closed mouth*. Easier said than done, when every muscle in the body and head says hit that baby now!

While there are an infinite number of variations, there are but three basic types of salmon rises. The most common is the hook, or curling rise. This occurs when the fish decides to grab what's offered, and it begins its interception with a waggle of the tail and raises its head to allow the current to lift it to the surface. As it reaches the correct position, just to one side or the other of the fly, it snaps its body to one side and takes the fly in at an angled attitude. Because most salmon, even the smaller grilse, are twenty-two inches and longer, when this sideways maneuver is put into motion, the tail or a portion of the back is frequently visible – just before the fly is actually mouthed. This is the most important nuance of salmon fishing. The practiced trout angler will invariably strike too soon. He'll strike at the show of tail or back, and while he may actually feel a tap on the line, the fish simply doesn't have the fly yet. With the wet fly, the conventional advice is not to do anything until resistance is felt . . . then tighten up. No sensible angler will argue with this generality.

The second most common rise is the simple head-and-tail-tipdown take. This is most apt to take place in calm water when the fish doesn't have a strong current to work against. It doesn't have to make that hook, or curl, to grab the fly and then move quickly to return to its former resting spot. It can simply drift up slowly, open its mouth, and drop down as it places its dorsal fins in the "dive" position. But here again, the dorsal fin is frequently seen before the fly is seized. Patience, friend, patience.

The third, and most uncommon, rise is the rushing rise that is best compared to Pickett's Charge at Gettysburg. It almost seems with this type of rise that the fish is mad as hell and destruction of the fly is what it has in mind. Rises like this have been known to make anglers soil their waders and splinter fine bamboo rods in the wink of an eye. It is wonderful to behold if your pacemaker has an overdrive gear. It is also the sort of strike that is either hooked solidly or not at all. But again, if your nerves are made of granite and you can actually see that mouth close on the fly . . . wet or dry . . . you'll have a better chance to see the rod tip bend.

With the hook rise, the fish is usually pretty serious about wanting that fly. If the light is right and you can spot the form of the salmon in the water, it's not difficult to see the mouth open and close. When it closes, take up the slack and give a solid pull to sink the barb. There will be a slight delay between the visual contact and the actual take. What happens (and I'm convinced of this) is that the salmon takes the fly initially between its lips and then does a double shuffle and jerks its head once more to drive the fly deeper into its mouth. How's that again?

Some ten years ago, on the Eagle River, while sitting on a rock changing flies, I noticed a small school of parr almost at my boot toe. The water was less than ten inches

This grilse finally "ate" a Bomber after rushing for it a dozen times. While fish after fish may charge the high-floating flies, hooking them can sometimes be challenging.

deep here, but there was a bit of current and the situation was a kind of micro–salmon pool. The tiny salmon were really excited about anything that drifted over them, and as I smacked a black fly on my wrist, I plucked the little devil between thumb and forefinger and flicked it into the water. A three-inch parr rose in a perfect hook rise and ate it. I'm sure my companions thought I was nuts because I fed a dozen black flies as well as some weed seeds and tiny specks of driftwood to that school of parr for the next hour. The weed seeds and wood would be ejected, but the black flies were eaten. A fascinating aspect of this fish-feeding operation was to note that while most of the parr took floating flies and imitations in the hook manner, an occasional parr rose head-and-tail fashion, and one crazy parr charged after anything à la Pickett's Charge!

But the most startling discovery was that each time these little fish would grab something, they would hold it for the blink of an eye and then *twist their heads* as they adjusted the black fly deeper into their mouths for swallowing!

I felt like shouting Eureka!, or something like that. Not only did adult salmon do precisely the same thing when grabbing a surface fly, but individual fish apparently acquired the tendency to rise one way or the other. And not only that (get ready for a dandy), some fish were decidedly *left-handed risers while others favored the right hook rise*. A few were ambidextrous risers, but most did indeed favor one side or the other. If you doubt this, spend fifteen minutes at a trout hatchery and watch an individual fish eat a dozen pellets. Shift your attention from one fish to another, and you'll see that each fish shows a preference for left- or right-finned feeding!

Can this have any application in practical angling? You bet it can, when a certain fish refuses your best offerings from your side of the river. On more than one occasion, I've changed casting positions and hooked an otherwise impossible fish. Just last season, I managed to stick an eighteen-pound salmon by casting over its nose to allow a Haystack dry fly to appear on his off side. A right-handed riser, pure and simple!

I do subscribe to the theory that adult salmon, upon entering fresh water, have some distant recall of eating a heap of surface food during their early lives as parr. Coming to the surface is no great trick for them if the current isn't too severe, and they can return to their lies without much effort. To the old angler's tale that adult salmon don't take real insects into their mouths, I say rubbish! I have watched far too many salmon rise up majestically and take caddis, stoneflies, and mayflies of all sizes with the confidence of a Letort brown. Now, what they do with these flies after they seize them is a total bafflement. The only substance I have ever found in a salmon's stomach in fresh water is a grayish green liquid with no solid material in it whatsoever!

As with wet flies, some dry fly patterns and shapes work better on certain rivers than others, but generally the winged Wulffs, Bivisibles of all colors, and Muddlers and Bombers – well dressed – will do the job. I added "well dressed," because I like to tie my salmon drys a bit sparser than most commercial versions. The more buoyant and high-riding a salmon dry is, the more difficult it is to hook fish. A fish of ten pounds or more pushes water ahead of it, and the high-riding fly is knocked out of the way at times. I prefer the wings to ride high, but the body of the fly ought to be *in* rather than *on* the water. Here again is a similarity with brown trout angling.

The most consistently productive dry fly for salmon I've used over the past four seasons has been a variation on the Haystack as tied by my friend Curt Hill of Philadelphia, Pennsylvania. Dubbed the CH, or Curt Hill, Haystack, it consists of nothing more than wings and tail of deer hair taken from the mask of the pelt and a body of cream-colored wool that Hill gathered on an Icelandic trip. I've used other sheep's wool and it works well, but the Icelandic wool wraps neatly around the hook and it floats like a cork. There is no hackle and the body rides perfectly on the surface. Fish don't usually play with this fly . . . they gulp it positively.

The Lee Wulff Surface Stone Fly, made with Lee's patented body system, is another approach to this "in-the-surface" presentation, which is the charm of the CH Haystack. There is hackle forward of the wing with Wulff's stonefly, but the weight of the molded body holds it tight to the surface instead of its being a high rider as are the usual Wulff series of dry flies, the powderpuffs, skaters, and such. I regularly carry both types of dry flies and both can be useful, sometimes on the same days on the same pools. The salmon that will show for the high-rider may not for the sparser-tied fly and vice versa. It must be remembered that the object is to get the salmon to rise or show for the fly in the first place. Every rise is not hooked, but nearly every fish that shows interest in something can be hooked. Note, I said *can* be hooked, not *will* be hooked. As your salmon fishing days become more numerous, this truth will be more evident.

The Bomber (a.k.a. Cigar-Butt, Shaggy Rat, etc.)

Fishing with a Bomber must be given at least a subheading under dry fly techniques in any modern discussion of Atlantic salmon fishing. While we can arrive at semi-logical reasons explaining why salmon rise for some floating flies and some sunken ones, the success of this tube of deer or caribou hair wound with a palmer hackle defies imagination. Legend has it that a disgusted angler once tossed his half-smoked cigar at a fish that wouldn't grab any of his flies, and lo, the salmon immediately grabbed the floating stub. An imitation of the discarded cigar butt was fashioned from clipped deer hair, so the story goes, and the fly was born. Variations of the Cigar-Butt soon followed and probably because of their size, some of them were christened "Bomber." To confuse fellow anglers (and fly tiers), some salmon chasers elected to call the fly "Shaggy Rat," hoping that others would think the fly they were using was a version of one of the famous Rat series.

Regardless of the origin, the first Bomber I saw in use was on the end of Norm Hathaway's leader at the pool where Ookpack (Owl) Brook flows into the Eagle River. One evening following dinner at Norm's camp, I walked down to the junction pool to have a few final casts. A sizable fish showed five or six times well behind my wet fly but seemed to have no desire to actually eat it. Norm was watching and asked if I minded if he had a try. I didn't, and he proceeded to tie on one of the ugliest creations I'd ever seen. It was a full three inches long, made of clipped caribou hair, and decorated with a full palmer hackle. I think the palmer hackle was white. The big thing did sound like a B-29 swishing back and forth as he extended his line, and I really thought the man was crazy. The big bug landed ten feet beyond the salmon's position, and he began to strip it back furiously through the choppy water. The fly was actually skipping from ripple to ripple when there was an explosion of white water. The salmon didn't get hooked, but Norm smiled and said, "Watch now, he'll get it the next time."

The same kind of cast, jerk, jerk, jerk, jerk, and pow! The fish made three huge bulges as Norm kept it moving, and on the third bulge, the Bomber was engulfed deep into the fish's mouth. A hard twenty-minute fight in the fast water, and I had the honor of tailing a fine sixteen-pound male fish. A dramatic introduction to the power of the Bomber.

Over the past twenty years, the Bomber (see photo in color section) has become standard fare on dozens of salmon rivers in Canada and Maine. It has taken fish that supposedly couldn't be caught and has risen thousands more that were eventually taken on other flies. It has also proven to be the ace in the hole on so many trips that might otherwise have been total flops that its reputation grows with each season. It isn't the cure-all (nor is anything), but it is a must in any serious salmon angler's fly box.

In spite of all the touting and wondrous tales told about the Bomber, the style of tie does have a serious drawback. It is damned hard to achieve a good ratio of fish hooked per fish that will rise to it. Atlantics can be mighty fussy about other types of flies, but when they're serious about eating a standard wet or traditional dry fly, they usually have it solid and that's that. There is absolutely nothing standard or usual about how a salmon rises for a Bomber. But they can tear their mouths open to such a degree that the huge fly is inhaled and still not get hooked. They can lunge and slash with such fury that anyone watching would swear by all that's holy that escaping the bug would be impossible. At other times they will come up slowly under the huge fly and bounce it playfully several times, like a seal playing with a ball, and never attempt to grab it.

A particular fish may chase a Bomber twenty times without touching it and at the twenty-first cast grab it so solidly there can be no question about the strike. When fish are in a Bomber "mood," there will be no shortage of excitement, even if a fish is not hooked.

Part of the problem in hooking fish on a Bomber is the construction of the fly itself. Properly tied on a long-shank hook, the Bomber is a mouthful for even a sizable fish of, say, ten or twelve pounds. Small versions of the Bomber, known as Buck Bugs,

Labrador Bugs, and the Ted Williams (yep, after the baseball player—in many parts of Canada he's much better known as a salmon fisher than a long-ball hitter), are much easier to hook fish with. They work well at times, but the full-size bomber, meaning one tied on a size 4 at least, is the "real" thing. I've used a Bomber as large as 1/0, and as a long-shank 1/0 fly it's somewhat more than difficult to cast. Into a stiff breeze it's impossible. I've tried a dozen or more hook styles searching for the ideal Bomber base and have yet to find one that I'd consider perfect. The Limerick bend is fine for regular flies, but the bushy hair that forms the long body usually fills the gap, preventing easy hooking. What's needed is a slightly wider gap and a short barb (or perhaps no barb) to facilitate quick penetration. As we've noted, the Bomber is a mouthful, and salmon seem to recognize quickly that this thing is not something to carry around in the mouth for any length of time. They can rise to a Bomber, take it in their mouths, and drop it before the angler can react. As with any fly, the strike shouldn't be made until the fish actually has it in the mouth . . . but with the Bomber, this is frequently impossible to determine. The best rule is to strike smartly when a Bomber can no longer be seen.

The fun and frustration of casting a Bomber was perfectly demonstrated by Carol Pierce on the Mecatina one afternoon. Known to the regulars of that river as "the General," Pierce loved the Bomber almost as much as he loved the river and its salmon. Not wanting the other guests to know what he caught most of his fish on, he carefully entered his catches in the camp log as being taken on the Shaggy Rat. But it was a Bomber he cast much of the time. We drew each other as fishing partners that day, and as was customary, we took turns working through the Sidewalk Pool. As I recall, I rose a couple of fish on my first run but failed to hook one. Watching this, he announced that he was going to try a Bomber in an attempt to "wake 'em up." Boy did he ever! Within a half-hour I believe every fish in the pool took a pass at his "Shaggy Rat." The boils and leaps and slashes were monumental. Fish flung themselves at the high-riding Bomber as he jerked and skittered it across the pool. It didn't seem to matter what he did. If the fly floated freely with no movement whatsoever, the fish still charged it like wild-eyed tackles zeroing in on a diminutive quarterback. Some fish actually leaped over the fly, and others boiled repeatedly as the fly bobbed and danced. I don't think Carol made a single cast that wasn't attacked. How many fish did he hook? Not one! But it certainly was fun to watch. After this exciting demonstration, which proved there were a lot of fish in the pool that day, we each took two fish on hitched wet flies of normal size . . . a 6 for this river.

Stories of this kind are common when Bombers are involved. Nearly every salmon angler who's tried them can report bizarre experiences. There's something about that cylindrical shape that can drive the salmon to do strange things. Many times they don't appear to be even trying to eat it, merely knocking it about and doing tricks with it. They will do odd things with any sort of fly when the notion strikes them, but with the Bomber there never seems to be a standard sort of behavior. We can't explain this in any way even approaching logic as we can with smaller or more traditional flies. There isn't anything in the ocean or fresh water that resembles a Bomber in silhouette or texture.

Where large brook trout coexist with Atlantic salmon, I've found that they too will devour a Bomber like it was the last supper when they're so inclined . . . which is almost always. And even where salmon don't appear, as on the Little Minipi River in Labrador, the trophy brookies there are keen for Bombers of the most outlandish proportions. A big brookie's mouth, however, is much larger than a salmon's of equal length and weight. The slower-growing north country brook trout can develop a massive head with a correspondingly mammoth maw. Bombers a full three inches long vanish in such a cavern, so when they decide to eat one, the trout have no trouble. I must add that Bombers of all sizes and colors are also excellent night-fishing producers on large brown trout and bass. Come to think of it, I've caught quite a few northern pike on them too.

I've not heard of Bombers being shown to European salmon (although someone must have tried it by this time), but I'd certainly like to introduce them to Irish and Scottish fish. I'm sure the gillies over there would be appalled at the sight of them, but who knows, they might work beautifully. I am sure, however, that on any North American salmon rivers I wouldn't want to be caught without a few Bombers in my kit. Plain old deer or caribou hair is my choice by far, with a reddish-brown hackle wound over. Second on the list would be a snow-white model with white hackle. The standard tie for Bombers calls for a tuft of woodchuck hair at the tail and another tuft of the same sticking out in front of the eye. This makes the Bomber appear the same, fore and aft. There's no need for this to be woodchuck hair, however; almost any tail or guard hairs will do the job. It's the clipped body that makes it float well after being dipped or rubbed liberally with fly dressing.

13

Of Guides and Sports

The disparities between salmon anglers are no less pronounced among those labeled "guides." The use of quotation marks is warranted today, and probably always has been, because a good number of otherwise fine folks wearing the title are simply not salmon guides. They are merely individuals who accompany the sport. On salmon rivers throughout the New World, the angler is always the *sport*— never the client, the guest, or the customer, at least as far as the guides are concerned. By the lodge owner some other label may be applied to those who are paying to fish, but never by the guide. In New Brunswick and Newfoundland, sport is always pronounced *spart* and Blue Charm is Blue *Chair-um*. Among the Scotch-Irish-English blend that prevails on many Canadian salmon rivers, the American ear sometimes has a hard time (that's *haird toim*) understanding how the letters *a* and *o* are used. There is no rule—one simply has to pay attention.

The foregoing provides a clue to how to recognize an authentic guide from his modern imitators. Age has something to do with it, but it's not a surefire indicator. I've fished with some extremely young guides who were the real thing and some old-timers who hadn't the foggiest notion about what Atlantic salmon fishing was all about. Some were pleasant companions on the river and some were not. Some knew the salmon lies like the inside of their closets while others were about as useful in pointing out good places to cast as is my neighbor's cat. As the old Major Hoople cartoon strip used to state so often, "Heros are made, not born!"

I am usually at ease with a Canadian salmon guide the first time I hear him say Blue Chair-um. I know he's got the right stuff in his blood to be good. He may or may not be top-notch, but the odds are good. Number of years spent on the river is also important, because then he will have seen runs of salmon come and go and should have his memory bank full of mental pictures covering where and when fish will respond. A good guide can make or break a salmon adventure.

Because most salmon fishing camps can't accommodate large numbers of anglers during any single week, a complement of a half-dozen guides is about the maximum number you'll encounter at any location. They'll come in all ages, sizes, temperaments, and skill levels. Unless you've been to the camp before or have quizzed someone who has, you won't have any idea who is the best guide, or which one will suit your personality and fishing style. An alert camp manager will sometimes make an effort to match angler and guide to personality, but it isn't always perfect. For example, some guides talk a lot and so do some anglers. It's a good idea to get the talkers together. Other guides avoid small talk like the plague, so matching them up with a quiet sport will usually work well. Not all guides are expert fly rodders, but some are better than any angler they've ever guided. The sport who's something of a duffer can benefit tremendously under the wing of a guide who doesn't mind doing some instructing. The hotshot sport who can cast into the middle of next week can, in turn, help a young guide who'd like to become more proficient with the tools of the game.

After a few years of watching groups of anglers come and go, most guides are exposed to a wide cross-section of sports. The good ones become very good at sizing up an angler's abilities and personal quirks with a few hours of riverside observation. They'll adjust their conversations to your whims and be of tremendous help if you allow them to. A few, for whom guiding salmon anglers is merely a summer diversion, never really get into the spirit of the thing and while they'll get you on the river and back again, won't stick with the job for more than a season or two. Some learn to love it, and when not engaged in their regular occupations give up money and comfort just to be on the river. It must be remembered that salmon fishing in most parts of Canada is an extremely short-term operation. On some rivers the season is a mere eight weeks, and even in the more southern waters three months covers the bulk of it. All guides must work at something else during the off-seasons in order to survive. Some wouldn't miss guiding for anything and have been at it most of their lives and will continue until they can no longer pull on their boots.

The kind of guide I enjoy is the one who himself likes to fish and who views the sport-guide relationship as that of a golfer and a savvy caddy. The golfer, or the angler, takes the shot or makes the cast and the caddy, or the guide, suggests approaches and which club or fly to use. The green-wise caddy has been there before and so has the salmon-wise guide. It's possible, if the angler has fished the river previously, to have a good understanding of the lies and how best to fish certain pools. The first-timer to any river is well advised to listen to the guide's advice at the outset and try it before making any judgments. A well-remembered example is worth recalling.

During my salad days of salmon chasing, I once waded into the tail end of a fine-looking pool and began casting to a submerged rock about sixty feet away. It looked like a likely spot—at the lip of a slick pool that lay above some fast water. It was an unfamiliar stretch of the Northwest Miramichi and my friend and guide, Earl Matchett, sat quietly on a rock watching me slash away. I stuck with the pool for twenty minutes without having a rise or seeing any movement and began to reel up, announcing to Earl, "Guess there's nothing here, let's move on up to another pool."

Earl chuckled and shook his head in disbelief, "Don't be too fast. Why don't you catch that fish right there in front of you?"

"Where?"

"It's layin' there about four feet below your rod tip and about six feet from the bank. If you'd taken another step downstream you'd-a stepped on it!"

I adjusted my polaroids, took a look at where he pointed and, sure enough, there *was* a salmon finning slowly in a small depression in the gravel, less than ten feet away. In my haste to prove I "knew" where the salmon ought to be in a strange pool, and to show off my casting ability as well, I had cast far beyond the hot spot for that particular time of the year. Earl explained later that the fish moved into the center of the pool as the water dropped, but at this height they loved to stick close to the bank, where the current was just right. After I swallowed a lump of pride, Earl advised me to move upstream about twenty feet and cast to the fish so that the fly would swing from the middle of the pool and coast toward the shore and over the fish. I did. It worked, and the nine-pound salmon took on the first cast. Earl allowed, after netting the fish, that he's seen close to a hundred salmon hooked in the same spot over a period of fifty years and most of them had risen for a fly cast in precisely the same way. When I asked Earl why he didn't offer the advice when I began fishing the pool, he replied, "Because you didn't ask for it!"

Another sport-guide exchange took place on the Eagle River when an excellent caster from Connecticut found himself with an Eskimo guide. Before heading down the river the sport had heard the guide conversing with the camp cook in their native Inuit. Assuming that the young man spoke little or no English, the sport began using what can best be referred to as "Hollywood Indian" jargon. "We go-um down river catchem big salmon, huh?"

The guide nodded in the affirmative.

When they got to the first pool the sport pointed to the river and said, "Me cast-um there?" The guide nodded again.

By and by, the sport hooked a fish, played it well, and in due time his guide expertly handtailed the salmon and carried it to shore. The sport wanted some photos of his first Eagle River salmon and began showing the Eskimo how to use his 35-millimeter camera. I was fishing the upper end of the same pool about seventy-five feet away but in the clear morning air I could hear the dialogue.

"See here, look-um in here and see me and salmon. Okay. Make picture clear by doing this. Push-um button here."

The guide stepped back, camera at the ready, and said, "Now, Mr. Clothier, if you'll just push your cap back a bit the shadow won't shield your face and we'll get a much nicer picture. Wait just a minute. I see you've got the film speed indicator set incorrectly for the 64 ASA film I saw you load. I've got a Nikon just like this and I forget sometimes myself."

The sport's mouth dropped open and he stammered, "You speak English!"

"Yes, I had to learn, since no one on the faculty at MIT understood Inuit."

Not all Atlantic salmon guides have attended MIT and coach anglers during the summer, but one should never assume that all guides are bumpkins. Their vocabularies and favorite conversational subjects may not match the sports', but they know their turf and some listening time will be valuable.

You'll come across the odd guide who won't respond to anything and really doesn't care about what he's doing. If the camp owner is about, try to change guides. If that isn't possible, make the best of it and promise yourself not to visit that camp again. But such total "clams" are in the minority and it's the rare guide who won't rise to the bait of being asked to share his expertise. Most of the time, it's the sport who creates the impasse, and the number-one mistake is to volunteer a lengthy history of your fishing career. It's a given that you must like to fish, otherwise you wouldn't be on a salmon stream in the first place. But what you did in Minnesota on your last walleye outing or how you're the terror of the bonefish flats in the Yucatan or some other faraway place won't cut any mustard with an Atlantic salmon guide. Until you prove you can cast to and hook a salmon, he won't be impressed with tales of previous derring-do. An angler's skill and understanding is quite obvious within an hour or so. And believe me, any salmon river guide *has* heard it all and seen the best and the worst over a half-dozen seasons.

A good guide should, first of all, know where the fish ought to be at all times of the season and direct his sport to the best possible spot for casting. He should keep his eye on the water and notify the sport when a fish has shown or flashed beneath the fly. If adjustment must be made in casting or location he should make a note of it. If the angler chooses not to take the advice, that's his business. The guide should suggest a

Only some fast footwork by the guide saved this grilse for Tom Goins. Hooked in a pool above this fast water, the fish decided to make a break by dashing into the foam. Sometimes all one can do is watch and weep!

change of flies when it seems appropriate and tie on a new one if the sport chooses. How much or little a guide helps on the first day is largely up to the angler. If he needs and wants the help, being shy about asking for it is a mistake.

Within a minute or so after hooking a fish, the sport should announce if the fish is to be killed or released. How the fish is netted or otherwise secured is important in either case. Minimal handling is preferable if the fish is going to be freed, with netting or beaching a last resort. If the angler wishes to handtail the fish himself, by all means make it clear that your decision is no reflection on his skill, it's simply a case of you wanting to do it yourself and if the fish is lost it's certainly not the guide's fault.

While it's traditional for guides to fish at some camps, it's not a widespread practice and certainly improper at best, and downright cheating in some cases. After all, the sport is the one who's paying for the rod time on the river, and salmon that the guide catches are fish the sport might have taken. On most salmon pools, the first angler to fish it on a new day stands the best chance to hook a fish. For a guide, with or without the sport's knowledge, to cast to the best lies first is simply not fair. Of course, many fish are hooked by guides with the rod then turned over to the sport for playing and landing. But your desire to do this should be announced long before you begin casting. In my opinion, the guide should never fish while doing his job unless invited to do so by the sport. He's not attending to business, and camp owners and managers should not allow it.

On the other hand, watching a sport goof up badly by not properly hooking several salmon, casting to the wrong spots, and otherwise missing good opportunities to raise fish can drive a guide nuts or worse. If he's a good salmon angler, as many of them are, it's frustrating to watch such antics day after day and not want to demonstrate his own skills. If a sport has fished through a pool and not had any takers, it's a good practice to offer the rod to the guide occasionally and ask him to have a crack at it. Some guides will refuse unless pressured and others will jump at the chance. Watch what they do, and if they hook a fish, it's your turn to play gillie if the guide wants the fish himself. Nine times out of ten they'll offer the rod to you for playing and landing, but they might want a grilse for dinner too. Hundreds of first-time salmon anglers have profited greatly by watching their guide cast to, hook, and land a salmon. The attentive beginner can learn more by watching carefully than he might from all of the books in the world–including this one.

At today's rates for Atlantic salmon fishing, ranging from one hundred dollars per day to nearly ten times as much on some fabled rivers (not counting the cost of getting there), tipping the guide is a small part of the overall price. The rules are not chiseled in stone but as a guideline ten dollars per day is standard procedure on most Canadian salmon rivers. At current exchange rates this is approaching fourteen dollars in Canadian funds. Five bucks a day brands a cheapskate, twenty-five dollars a day is extravagant. A tad more than ten dollars is proper if the guide has performed good service and

Drifting and casting here and there is a restful way to fish a salmon river—if you're guided by a boatman who can handle a pole and canoe. Guy Silliker is one of the best.

was a good partner as well. It's not necessary to make a big show of it, but guides also appreciate an item of tackle or other gift. Be sure to ask the lodge owner if he approves of this, especially if the gift happens to be alcoholic in nature. Some camp owners have rigid rules about booze and guides and the guest must pay careful attention to them.

Inquiry should also be made about offering your guide a drink at day's end or on the river. Some sports carry hip flasks of their favorite elixir while fishing, which can cloud reflexes and fishing ability, and too much can be downright dangerous if wading in swift water is called for or angling is done from a boat. If the camp owner says it's okay to offer the guide a friendly nip to toast a fish, fine. But it's always best to confine the serious drinking to your cabin or room at day's end.

14

What Are the Odds?

Partial fish don't compute with most anglers, unless those anglers happen to be biologists or computer buffs. To understand today's salmon success ratios we must speak in the language of decimal points. On New Brunswick's famous Miramichi, perhaps the best known Atlantic salmon river system in the world, 1985 saw anglers harvest .43 salmon per day. Of the twenty thousand or so licensed sports flinging their flies, plus an uncounted few thousand more doing so without benefit of legal paper, that figure doesn't amount to many salmon steaks per angler. But, as with fishing of all sorts, some do much better than others. In order for a half-fish average to be maintained, some fishermen must catch several while others catch none. I'd consider any Atlantic salmon trip worth the effort for a result of one fish per day, or six for the week. My salmon logs reveal lows of zero to a high of forty-one fish for six days of fishing, and every other number in between. Yes, I've blanked out more than once, usually due to no fish being in the river at hand. Such weeks can throw a terrible negative factor into the calculations. But even with the no-fish trips, thirty years of chasing these wonderful fish have resulted in a slightly better than one-fish-per-day average. All but the greediest of anglers should be happy with that.

Every imaginable natural and manufactured handicap can affect the outcome of a salmon adventure. Weather, moon phase, tide strength, river condition, tackle, guide, personal casting ability, leaky waders, eyesight . . . the list is endless. But all that aside, the angler who can manage a forty-foot cast, is reasonably well equipped, and on the river at a *good* time ought to catch an Atlantic salmon. What's a good time? It's when the fish are in the river in "bright" condition and you happen to be there.

Unlike many trout streams and bass lakes, salmon may only be caught at the time they are in the river but there is an optimum period. Once a salmon settles in for spawning chores and its flanks turn reddish brown (and the water is usually lower), fishing becomes exceedingly difficult. In most salmon rivers on the North American continent the salmon bright season is of short duration: six weeks on some rivers and seldom more than eight weeks on the best of them. A few rivers have "early" runs of fish and a few more have "late" runs. On certain rivers these early and late runs may bear the largest fish that enter the river, but there won't be many of them. The only way the angler lacking experience can find out when to be present is to trust the camp owner or quiz as many Atlantic salmon fishers as possible to find out when the action is best. Being businesspeople, some camp owners and managers are not above a bit of hyperbole when telling of the fishing success enjoyed at their establishments. I can't fault them for honest salesmanship, but if a camp owner tells you over the phone or you read in the brochure that "nearly everyone limits out on old 'Nevermiss' river," be leery. Ask for references, and by all means follow up on them. Conversely, don't be a total skeptic, because conditions can turn around quickly and you could miss out on something wonderful.

I almost canceled a trip to the upper Eagle River in Labrador one year because of reports of extremely low water. I went anyway and the reports were right. When we stepped out of the Cessna float plane at Norm Hathaway's camp I wondered if there would be enough water at the end of the week to allow a takeoff. I'm not kidding, I was really concerned!

I found some small pleasure in catching pan-sized brook trout in a couple of spring holes along the shore of the normally brawling river the next day, but I was having serious doubts about being there. This state of affairs changed abruptly the next morning when the sky changed from blue to black and tanks of rain fell for eighteen hours. The river jumped a foot overnight, and salmon a few pools downstream charged into the camp's water in astounding numbers. We caught fish in numbers for the remaining four days of our trip. It seemed the salmon were tired of the low water too, and nearly any fly that floated over them was seized with a vengeance. A side note to this trip is that a first-timer was among the guests and he remarked that all he had read about the sport was a lot of poppycock.

"Game fish. Are you kidding? I caught seven in one morning and quit fishing at noon because it was so easy!"

The other guests chided him about this, explaining that he might not find it so easy the next time. He didn't. At last report this same one-trip expert made five more Atlantic safaris before finding himself attached to another fish. It may sound snobbish, but fledgling salmon anglers are well advised to keep their mouths shut during the first half-dozen outings. Today's truth will be tomorrow's folly.

The large number of good salmon rivers in the provinces of Quebec and New Brunswick make those general destinations serious considerations. In broad terms, the rivers of the Gaspé give up larger fish, but the North Shore rivers (North Shore of the St. Lawrence River) produce more fish per man hour of angling. The Gaspé rivers are also more expensive than the more distant rivers of the North Shore, but the additional cost of flying into the latter adds to the price. New Brunswick rivers can be driven to for the most part and, because of this, are not so costly per week of fishing.

Fishing on the island of Newfoundland will also see close to a fish per day of angling during a good run. A large percentage of these rivers can also be driven to, but that also means more anglers because in Newfoundland by law there is no "private" fishing. However, the topography and "understanding" in certain locales precludes too much public infringement on camp waters. Labrador, which is a part of Newfoundland, offers the most remote Atlantic salmon fishing in the free world. Practically all Labrador salmon rivers must be reached by small airplanes on floats. One should never book a Labrador salmon trip if sticking to a tight schedule is necessary. The chances of being fogged in coming or going (or both) is a distinct possibility. But do it if you can, because the experience of fishing where the only humans you'll see on the stream will be the other people in your camp is worth the time.

All comments about Labrador apply to the northern region of Quebec, or Nuevo Quebec. This is the Ungava Bay drainage and there flow the mighty George and Whale Rivers. This is Inuit country and during the course of a week in August (the best fishing month) you'll see at least one snow flurry. You'll also average that fish per day, which seems to be the magic number everywhere. It is home to the largest herds of caribou east of Alaska and for the wolves that follow them. In some sections of the major rivers in the Ungava the Arctic char are plentiful. For fish to eat while in camp, I suggest char before salmon. Lover of salmon that I am, on the fly and on the plate, there is nothing in this world that remotely suggests the luscious flavor of fresh char. Since this fish seldom, if ever, finds its way to a fish market, the angler should sample the bounty!

The price paid for Atlantic salmon fishing at this writing varies from a low of one hundred dollars to one thousand dollars per day. It can go much higher in Europe and astronomically higher in Norway, but from all data I've seen, that one-fish-per-day rule applies everywhere. The higher dollar value is usually on rivers where larger fish are the norm, but there are fewer of them. What it comes down to is this: you can catch more fish at a lower rate—but they'll be smaller, grilse mostly. Or, you can pay the higher fee and take your chances at latching onto a big fish of twenty pounds or more—but you won't catch many of them and you may not catch one at all. Are you a trophy hunter or do you want lots of action? It's a tough choice, but I usually opt for the action.

15

Odds and Ends— About Gear and Such

O ne of the nicest things about writing a book like this is having the chance to ramble on about what I think is important and lightly touch on the less important. Well, perhaps such things as waders, flyboxes, vests, socks, and sundries are important, but they are not of captivating interest. I have lived long enough and fished enough hours to have formed some dogmatic opinions and I'll now share some of them with you. Few readers will give a hoot about these opinions because, like me, they've probably decided on what "odds and ends" they prefer and are just as opinionated as I am. It's great fun to be shocking at times, so I'll now be just that.

Fly boxes. Frankly, there really aren't many good ones on the market and never have been. Dry flies are served well with the multicompartmented plastic ones pioneered by the Bill DeWitt Company some fifty years ago. Wet flies were kept in sheepskin books by many of our grandfathers but eventually all of the hooks rusted and when wool gets wet it won't dry totally for at least three weeks. Those expensive Wheatley fly boxes from England are lovely to look at with full rows of classic or hairwing salmon flies. But the clips eventually wear out and rust (we can't keep them dry forever) and four of them in a vest weigh three hundred pounds at day's end. The Wheatleys are just dandy for storing flies or for show-off time, but on the stream they're a bother. They also sink like a rock if you drop one while wading. Far better for stream use are the soft plastic boxes supplied with Shakespeare fly lines. I'm not sure if that company still uses these boxes but snooping around tackle stores and friends' garages may still turn up one or two. Glue some squares of rubber foam inside and stick your salmon flies there. I have a half dozen of these boxes and they're the best imaginable. They last forever, float if dropped, and each one will hold fifty flies or more. Six of them, full of flies, don't weigh a pound.

Vests. Any angler who buys a vest without measuring the pockets to discover if they'll actually accept his fly boxes is asking for trouble. The trouble begins with the manufacturers who apparently don't fish. The outside pockets of seventy-five percent of today's fishing vests aren't large enough to hold a Wheatley fly box or one of my home-altered plastic boxes. Any vest that *will* carry your boxes and that has a large pocket in the rear for a rain jacket is acceptable. Some anglers dislike Velcro closures but, for my money, this modern material beats buttons and zippers hands down. It won't rust, fall off, or snag loose coils of line.

Waders. For traveling light, the flyweight waders from Red Ball are the best I've found. They're reasonably tear-resistant and will last for four seasons with casual care. You'll need wading shoes with these (and with other stocking-foot waders), and buy felt soles–always. Cleated soles are no good on any salmon river I've fished. The best felt soles are those with small metal rivets imbedded into the soft material. Boot-foot waders are easier to put on and take off but they're also heavier and less comfortable to walk in. They are, however, warmer than stocking-foot models. If the water you expect to be wading in is below the fifty-five-degree mark, you'll need longjohns. Forget hip-high boots. They're for guides and trout fishermen.

Hats. Wear any sort of hat you like for picture purposes or personal statement, but be sure to have some sort of wool cap that fits close to the head. Anything else will blow off the noggin at least twice during any salmon fishing day–I've never seen a salmon river where the wind doesn't blow. If you must wear a fedora or western lid, afix a chin strap.

Glasses. Don't even consider embarking on a salmon trip without Polaroid sunglasses, or clip-ons that fit over your regular glasses if you wear them. You'll see fifty percent better on bright days and one hundred percent better when it's necessary to look into the water at netting or tailing time. Buy one of those elastic bands that goes around the back of the head to keep glasses on your face and out of the river.

Wading staff. If you're not totally sure of your wading ability, use a wading staff in broken water. Commercial models are for sale but your guide will be happy to cut one for you at streamside. If you drop or lose a local model, it's an easy matter to find another one.

Sylvia is obviously happy about seeing this fish in the net, but she and the guide have to be careful about jumping from rock to rock. Felt soles on wading shoes and boots are a must for salmon fishing on any river.

Insect repellent. Every salmon river in Canada has black flies. Some have black flies and mosquitoes. Both insects are fond of salmon fishermen, and unless you have skin as thick as elephant ears, you will be attacked. Insect repellents containing at least twenty-five percent N-diethyl-m-toluamide (deet) are the only ones to consider. All others don't have enough oomph to keep the little beggars away. Rub the backs of your hands and all exposed skin, and smear a dollop on hat and shirt sleeves *before* going on the stream. Try to keep the stuff out of your eyes and away from watch crystals, and wipe the palms of your hands on a paper towel before handling fly line. Insect repellents that keep the bugs away will also melt fly-line coatings and most other plastics. Be especially careful with eyeglass frames and plastic lenses. I've made several eyeglass manufacturers rich over the years.

Another full-length book could be written about outdoor clothing, but the essence of the matter is stated in one line stolen from writer Boyd Pfeiffer: "Count on every adventure to be wetter, colder, or hotter than you expected and pack accordingly." Boyd is absolutely right. Three musts. You must carry at least three pairs of dry socks. You must carry a rain jacket. You must have a lightweight insulated jacket. Aside from that, you're on your own.

16

Caring For and Cooking the Catch

nglers are releasing a large percentage of their catch these days (and well they should), but there is nothing immoral about plunking a few in the freezer. The best Atlantic salmon you'll ever eat are those that go into the poacher within hours of being caught—the sooner the better. It is an unarguable fact that the best fish for the table is the freshest fish. But for a variety of reasons, all fish we catch cannot be consumed at the time of catching or even soon after. If the camp you're fishing from has a freezer, the quicker the fish is in it the better the taste will be later. All fish flesh begins to deteriorate the second it dies, but this process is delayed by fast freezing.

It is not necessary or desirable to scale or remove the entrails from an Atlantic salmon caught in fresh water. I'm sure that statement will raise the eyebrows of many anglers and chefs but it is absolutely true. To do so means poor-tasting fish and possible contamination. Since Atlantic salmon do not swallow solid food while on their spawning journey upstream, there is nothing in their stomachs being digested. To open up the body cavity is to invite the entrance of bacteria. Scraping the scales off can also cause harm by nicking or cutting the skin, allowing the same thing to happen. The interlocked scales and an unopened belly keep the fish in a natural sealed package. I do, however, cut out the bright red gills as soon as the salmon is killed. This allows the fish to bleed out and prevents the first stages of spoilage, which begins with the gills. My procedure is to quickly bop the fish on the head with a "priest," then cut the gills away with two incisions at the arch of the gills—where the two sides join. Do not remove the head or sever the backbone while doing this.

At camp, wrap the fish in plastic and lay it flat in the freezer. Laying it flat is very important because a crooked frozen fish is difficult to transport or slice into steaks. A serious discussion with careless guides will correct this problem when the first fish is dispatched. In some parts of Canada and Europe guides and gillies are still anxious to gut and scale Atlantic salmon. Don't allow them to do it. You'll be rewarded with much better tasting salmon.

Most salmon camps provide, or have for sale, plastic boxes and cardboard sleeves for transporting frozen salmon. Unless run over with a steamroller, these cartons will survive the trip to your final destination. There, wrap the fish with a second layer of freezer paper and seal well, using the "drugstore wrap." Bind this second wrapping with freezer tape and write the weight and date on each package. Thus wrapped, Atlantic salmon will keep well in a zero-degree freezer for six months. I've poached salmon that have been in the freezer for a full year and they still tasted quite good. There is some loss of flavor, but Atlantics keep amazingly well, much better than any other fatty fish I'm familiar with.

When you're ready to eat a frozen salmon, take it out of the freezer the night before the feast and allow it to begin thawing. By pressing on the package from time to time you'll know when to eviscerate it. When the package and flesh can be depressed slightly, unwrap it and make a slit from vent to throat. The entire abdominal contents can be plucked out in one still-frozen lump. If done correctly, there won't be a spot of blood on your fingers. The blood line that clings to the bottom on the backbone can be stripped clean with a teaspoon. Give the fish a quick swash under cold water and blot it dry with a paper towel, inside and out. Allow the fish to continue thawing until cooking time.

While I'll not attempt to list full recipes for Atlantic salmon in this book (because I would infringe on my wife Sylvia's cookbook sales), I will explain my three favorite methods of preparing them. The first and finest is poaching, which means cooking in boiling bouillon. There are umpteen things that could be added to the bouillon, but an onion, celery, and splash of dry white wine is all that's really important.

Into a fish poacher, place the onion, cut-up celery, and a cup of wine. Add enough water to cover the fish, and bring all to a boil. Slip the whole cleaned fish into the water and the rapid boil will stop. When it resumes boiling, reduce the heat to a gentle simmer and mix a drink. Set the timer for twenty-three minutes and when it buzzes the salmon will be done. With two spatulas remove the salmon, being careful not to break it, and deposit it gently onto a folded newspaper. Strip the skin away with a table fork from the upside and slide the flesh onto a fish-shaped platter. Decorate with greenery such as watercress, Bibb lettuce, lemon slices, and, of course, an olive in the eye socket. *Voilà!*

If you don't have or can't borrow a fish poacher of twenty-four inches or longer, a large roasting pan will do the job well.

Serving a poached salmon is easy and elegant. Simply remove chunks from the upper and lower halves of meat on either side of the lateral line and your guests will ooh and aah with an anticipatory drool. They'll love the fresh taste of salmon and the basic sauce, which can be lied about. Call it an old family secret if you wish, but don't tell them until much later that it consists of two parts mayonnaise to one part prepared mustard with a teaspoon of dill weed, a tablespoon of lemon juice, and a couple shakes of steak sauce. That's all. Sylvia goes into much more detail in her book, *Cleaning and Cooking Fish* (Hunting and Fishing Library, 1985), but since I poach most of the salmon at our house I'm entitled to these abbreviated directions.

Broiling can be done with steaks or fillets. I prefer the steaks because it's easier to cut a full "round" from a salmon carcass. Begin behind the head and cut even slices about an inch-and-a-half thick, severing the backbone and skin. Trim off a quarter inch of belly meat and you'll remove most of the fat and any unpleasant looking material. Brush both sides of the steaks with butter or cooking oil and place on the broiler rack that you've already covered with aluminum foil. Broil about four inches from the heat source for five-and-a-half minutes on a side. When served, the skin will pull off in one strip and can be enjoyed by the nearest available dog.

Baked salmon is also easy to prepare if you enjoy a stronger fish taste. Place the cleaned salmon on a sheet of heavy-duty aluminum foil and brush it inside and out with a solution of melted butter, chopped parsley, and a tablespoon of savory. Seal the foil around the fish and bake in a preheated oven for twelve minutes per pound at 350 degrees F. A tangy sauce consists of two tablespoons of steak sauce, two teaspoons of horseradish, and a cup of sour cream.

To properly enjoy Atlantic salmon, the predinner festivities should include a very dry martini or other favorite attitude-adjustment elixir, and the person responsible for catching the fish should be allowed, even encouraged, to recount the capture. The proper wine would be a Pinot chardonnay or a dry California chenin blanc. Many Rieslings are too sweet for my taste with salmon, although you may prefer them, and so are most of the rosés except for some of the West Coast pink wines made from Zinfandel grapes.

Regardless of your choice of wine or before-dinner cocktail, at some time during the Atlantic salmon dinner a special toast must be made. It is done the world over and if forgotten the fishing gods will "call you home" quickly. The toast must be "To the salmon." And it must be made with sincerity because the fish made the ultimate sacrifice for the meal!

17

The Areas and the Outfitters

Owners change, camps close, and laws vary from year to year—sometimes more frequently. The author cannot vouch for the comfort and quality of all facilities listed here. To recommend one camp over another would be unfair for a number of political and personal reasons. In contacting any of them, it's suggested that you ask for references from previous guests who live near you. Follow up on them. Also, ask the lodge owner any questions you might have about the fishing, the meals, the guides, and extra services. In most cases, the lodge owner can also answer questions about current seasons and regulations. For additional information, call the numbers listed under the individual province headings.

NOVA SCOTIA

Season: The salmon angling season varies throughout the province, but most of June through September is open season. Variation orders may be enacted on a temporary basis to take into account factors such as water levels and fish stocks. For up-to-date variation order changes, please contact the Department of Fisheries and Oceans, 902-426-5952.

Tagging: All persons who purchase a salmon license will receive a total of ten tags. All salmon caught and retained must immediately be tagged through the mouth and gill cavity with a tag whose number corresponds with the license number of the angler who caught the fish. For children thirteen years and under, the tag number must correspond to the license number of the person accompanying them. The tag must be securely locked.

When fishing, no one can possess a used or altered salmon tag or a tag that does not correspond to his or her license number. Possession of an untagged salmon is illegal. The tag must remain on the salmon until that salmon is prepared for consumption.

Location: The following table, compiled by some of Nova Scotia's top salmon fishermen, lists the best rivers and optimum fishing dates for salmon angling in Nova Scotia.

County and River	Fishing Dates	Best Period
Annapolis County		
Annapolis River	August 15–October 29	September 15–October 15
Colchester County		
Debert River	August 15–October 29	September 15–October 15
Economy River	August 15–October 29	September 15–October 15
Folly River	August 15–October 29	September 15–October 15
Stewiacke River	August 15–October 29	September 15–October 15
Cumberland County		
Maccan River	September 15–October 15	October 1–October 15
River Phillip	September 1–October 29	October 1–October 15
Wallace River	September 1–October 29	October 1–October 15
Digby County		
Salmon River	June 1–July 15	June 15–July 10
Guysborough County		
Ecum Secum River	June 1–August 29	June 20–July 31
Liscomb River	June 1–August 29	June 20–August 15
St. Mary's River	May 18–August 29	June 10–August 15
Salmon River	June 15–July 31	June 20–July 10

Halifax County
Ingram River	June 1–July 15	June 1–June 30
Moser River	June 1–August 29	June 20–July 31
Musquodoboit River	June 1–July 31	June 1–July 15
Salmon River	June 15–July 31	June 20–July 31

Hants County
Shubenacadie	August 15–October 15	September 15–October 15

Inverness County
Margaree River	June 1–October 15	September 1–October 15

Kings County
Gaspereau River	June 1–July 1	June 1–June 15

Lunenburg County
Gold River	May 10–July 31	June 1–June 30
LaHave River	May 10–July 31	June 1–July 31
Petite Riviere	June 1–August 30	June 1–June 30

Queens County
Medway River	May 10–July 31	June 1–July 1
Mersey River	June 1–July 31	June 1–June 20

Richmond County
Grand River	June 15–October 15	July 1–September 30

Shelburne County
Clyde River	June 1–July 15	June 10–June 30
Jordan River	June 1–July 15	June 10–June 30
Roseway River	June 1–July 15	June 10–June 30

Victoria County
Baddeck River	September 1–October 15	September 15–October 15
Middle River	September 1–October 15	September 15–October 15
North River	June 15–September 30	June 15–September 30

Fishing Licenses: Fishing licenses are available from all district offices of the Department of Lands and Forests and from vendors throughout the province, including most sporting goods stores. The fee is five dollars for a resident of Nova Scotia and twenty dollars for a non-resident. Fishing national parks requires a transferable National Parks Fishing License, available at park offices for ten dollars. Major changes are anticipated in the salmon angling license structure. Please check the summary provided by the Department of Lands and Forests, or write P.O. Box 68, Truro, Nova Scotia B2N 5B8.

Fishing Outfitters:

Atlantic Salmon Fly Shop, Margaree Forks, Nova Scotia B0E 2A0. Complete outfitters for Atlantic salmon. Fishing equipment available upon advanced request. Your host, Ronald Haldeman. Phone 902-248-2920.

Beaver Island Lodge Outfitters, Don Breen, P.O. Box 402, Milton, Queens County, Nova Scotia B0T 1T0. Ten miles west of Liverpool on Ten Mile Lake. Salmon fishing on two of Nova Scotia's best rivers (Medway, LaHave), brook and brown trout fishing on many of the numerous lakes and rivers in the area. Clean, modern accommodations, shower and bath, home-cooked meals. Remote, quiet wilderness. Member of the Professional Fishing and Hunting Outfitters Association of Nova Scotia, and the Professional Guides Association. Phone 902-354-4354.

Eastern Valley Outfitters, Aubrey and Carol Beaver, Sherbrooke, Guysborough County, Nova Scotia B0J 3C0. Complete outfitters for trout and Atlantic salmon fishing. Advance inquiries a must. Licensed guide available upon request. Members of the Professional Guides Association. Phone 902-522-2235.

Lansdowne Lodge, Tom and Marion Kennedy, Upper Stewiacke, Colchester County, Nova Scotia B0N 2P0. Complete outfitters for Atlantic salmon fishing. Specializing in fishing the Stewiacke, one of the best-producing rivers in Nova Scotia. Combine salmon fishing and upland bird hunting the first two weeks in October. Season August 1–October 15. Phone, collect, 902-268-2749.

Liscombe Lodge, Liscomb Mills, Guysborough County, Nova Scotia B0J 2A0. (Winter address: P.O. Box 456, Halifax, Nova Scotia B3J 2R5.) Complete outfitters for Atlantic salmon and trout fishing. Phone 902-779-2307; winter -425-5000. Telex #019-23525.

North Mountain Outfitters, Anna and Roger Ehrenfeld, Box 149, Middleton, Nova Scotia B0S 1P0. Facilities located at Trout Lake, Annapolis County, about 24 km (15 miles) south of Middleton on Route 10. Complete outfitters, and fully equipped for freshwater fishing (salmon/trout). Members of the Professional Guides Association. Phone 902-825-4030 day, or -825-6629 evening.

River View Lodge, Moyal Conrad, Greenfield, Queens County, Nova Scotia B0T 1E0. Situated on the Medway River, one of Nova Scotia's most prolific Atlantic salmon rivers. Also excellent trout fishing in the many brooks, streams, and lakes in the area. Clean accommodations include double and single rooms, showers, main living room, sauna, and a dining room serving home-cooked meals. Transportation supplied to and from the Greenfield Airport (small sport planes), two miles from the lodge. All equipment available for excellent salmon and trout fishing. Member of the Professional Fishing and Hunting Outfitters Association of Nova Scotia. Phone 902-685-2378 or -685-2376.

Sentinel Safety Consultants, Ron Seney, P.O. Box 1523, Wolfville, Nova Scotia B0P 1Z0. Outfitter for trout and salmon in Lunenburg County. Phone 902-275-4663.

Upper Musquodoboit River Valley Outfitter, Mike Boon, RR #1, Upper Musquodoboit, Halifax County, Nova Scotia B0N 2M0. Lodge located 24 km (15 miles) from Halifax International Airport on the Old Guysborough Road. Transportation provided to and from the airport. Salmon and sea run brook trout in the Musquodoboit, Stewiacke, Shubenacadie, and St. Mary's rivers. Member of the Professional Guides Association. Phone 902-568-2404.

For additional information, consult the 1986 Sports Fishing Summary of Regulations provided by the Nova Scotia Department of Lands and Forests, P.O. Box 68, Truro, Nova Scotia.

NEW BRUNSWICK
General Information:
No person shall kill or retain Atlantic salmon fry, parr, or smolt.
No person shall angle for Atlantic salmon except by fly fishing with an artificial fly.
No person shall angle for Atlantic salmon unless they are in possession of a valid license and tags for Atlantic salmon.
No person shall be in possession of Atlantic salmon tags that do not correspond to their angling license.
No person shall be in possession of a used or mutilated Atlantic salmon tag.
No person shall be in possession of an Atlantic salmon that is not properly tagged.
No person shall fish for Atlantic salmon by trolling.

Bag Limit: Ten fish per season (grilse only); six grilse in possession; two grilse per day. Anglers must stop fishing once they have retained the daily limit, or have released a maximum number of fish equal to twice the daily limit.

Hook and Release: Present New Brunswick federal angling regulations require the immediate live release of all angled, large Atlantic salmon greater than 63 cm (25 inches). The released, unharmed fish help rebuild threatened salmon runs; a released salmon will continue upstream to spawn and possibly provide sport for other anglers along the way. Also, it does not count toward season limit, meaning more angling for the releasing fisherman too.

Bright Salmon Seasons:

Waters tributary to the Bay of Chaleur: General season for bright salmon, June 8–September 30, with the following exceptions—

River	Season
Benjamin	July 1–October 15
Caraquet	July 1–October 15
Charlo	July 1–October 15
Eel	July 1–October 15
Jacquet	July 1–October 15
Middle	July 1–October 15
Nepisiguit	June 8–October 7
Pokemouche	July 1–October 15
Restigouche System	June 1–August 31
Tetagouche	July 1–October 15
Tracadie	July 1–October 15

Waters tributary to Northumberland Strait: General season for bright salmon, June 8–September 30, with the following exceptions—

River	Season
Bartholomew	Closed
Bartibog	July 1–October 15
Buctouche	July 1–October 15
Cains	July 1–October 15
Cocagne	July 1–October 15
Dungarvon (above Underwood Brook)	June 8–September 15
Little Southwest Miramichi (above Catamaran Brook)	June 15–September 15
Main Southwest Miramichi (above McKeil Brook)	June 8–September 15
Northwest Miramichi (above Little River)	June 8–August 31
Renous (above North Renous)	June 8–September 15
Rocky Brook	June 1–August 31
Sevogle (above Square Forks)	June 8–September 15

| Tabusintac | July 1–October 26 |
| Other tributaries of Main Southwest Miramichi (above Cains River, except Rocky Brook) | June 8–September 15 |

Waters tributary to the Bay of Fundy: General season for bright salmon, June 15–October 15, with the following exceptions—

River	Season
Alma River	June 15–October 15
Big Salmon (upstream of and including Walton Dam Pool)	June 15–September 15
Big Salmon (downstream from Walton Dam Pool)	June 8–October 22
Digdequash	June 15–October 15
Hammond (below French Village Bridge)	June 15–October 31
Hammond (upstream from French Village Bridge)	June 15–October 15
Kennebecasis	June 15–October 31
Keswick	June 15–October 15
Magaguadavic	June 15–October 15
Nashwaak (upstream from the Bridge at Stanley)	June 15–September 30
Nashwaak (downstream from the Bridge at Stanley)	June 15–October 15
Petitcodiac River System	August 15–October 15
Point Wolfe	Closed
Saint John (upstream from the Grafton Bridge at Woodstock)	June 15–September 30
Saint John (downstream from the Grafton Bridge at Woodstock)	June 1–October 15
St. Croix	June 15–September 15
Tobique	June 15–September 15

Outfitters Offering Atlantic Salmon Fishing:

Albert County

Fundy Outfitters, Malcolm Rossiter, P.O. Box 16, Hillsborough, New Brunswick E0A 1X0. 506-734-2424. Off Route 114 at Alma, on Forty-Five Road. Exit 430 Fundy National Park. One lodge, six guests, mixed groups, flush toilets, shower, boats, guide.

Rivers Inlet Lodge, Grant I. Woodworth, RR #1, Albert, New Brunswick E0A 1A0. Along Shepody River near Albert on Route 114. Exit 430, 488A, 504A, off Routes 2 and 6. Hunting and fishing lodge, three units, mixed groups, full-time guide, boats, showers, flush toilets.

Carleton County

Deerville Camps, W. Alton Morrison, RR #1, Lakeville, New Brunswick E0J 1S0. 506-276-3235. Lakeville, RR #1, along Route 560 at Deerville, exit at Centreville. One lodge, one cottage, twelve guests, mixed groups, dining room, flushes, showers, canoes, guide.

Governor's Table Camps, Hugh B. Smith and Gerald B. Shaw, Box 282, Hartland, New Brunswick E0J 1N0. 506-246-5466/375-6463. Juniper, Route 107, exit 153 from Route 2 on Route 107. One lodge, four cottages, twelve guests, mixed groups, dining room, fridges, showers, indoor toilets, electricity, TV, telephone, C.B. radio, guides, canoes, bow hunting.

Guimac Camps, Ralph Orser, RR #4, Hartland, New Brunswick E0J 1N0. 506-375-6268. Hartland area, 23 km (14 miles) from Hartland, off Route 104 at Becaguimec Stream. Four cottages, fifteen guests, mixed groups, dining room, no bedding, showers, indoor toilets, electricity, propane gas, telephone, guides, bow hunting, canoes.

Herb's Sporting, Herbert Pryor, P.O. Box 83, Centreville, New Brunswick E0J 1H0. 506-276-4768. Centreville, Route 560 off Route 110. One lodge, six guests, mixed groups, bath, showers, flush toilets, boats, guide.

Gordon D. Hill, RR #4, Hartland, New Brunswick E0J 1N0. 506-375-6488. Route 104, Hartland, exit 170 off Route 2, 19 km (12 miles) east of Hartland on Route 104. One lodge and family home, four guests, dining room, kitchen with electric stove in lodge, indoor (home) and outdoor (lodge) toilets, telephone, guides, one boat.

Juniper Lodge, Frank MacDonald (manager), Juniper, New Brunswick E0J 1P0. 506-246-5223. Juniper, Route 107. One lodge, twelve guests, mixed groups, bath, showers, flush toilets, electricity, telephone, kennels, bow hunting, boats, guides, canoeing, snowmobiling, cross-country skiing, snowshoeing.

Manuel's Hunting and Fishing Camps, Dale and Sheldon Manuel, RR #1, Hartland, New Brunswick E0J 1N0. Home: 506-375-8812/375-8840; camp: 506-375-6197. South Knowlesville, Hartland area, Exit 170 from Route 2, then from Route 104 to Knowlesville 19 km (12 miles). Lodge and cabins, showers, flush toilets, fridges, electricity and telephone, sixteen guests, mixed groups, guide, bow and black powder hunting.

Miramichi Camps, Earl F. Boyd, Juniper, New Brunswick E0J 1P0. 506-246-5291. Juniper area, 8 km (5 miles) from Juniper on Route 107. One lodge, four cottages, twelve guests, mixed groups, dining room, showers, indoor toilets, electricity, telephone, guides, three canoes, kennels, bow hunting.

Charlotte County

Andy's Cabin, Andrew Mosher, RR #3, Ledge Road, St. Stephen, New Brunswick E3L 2Y1. 506-466-5755. Piskahegan, Route 770. Cabin, shower, flush toilet, mixed groups, guide, boats.

Cranberry Lake Lodge, Leonary H. Way, RR #4, St. Stephen, New Brunswick E3L 2Y2. 506-466-3646/466-2015. Moores Mills, Route 3. Lodge, shower, dry toilets, three units, mixed groups, guide, four boats.

Mohannes Camp, Wilfred M. Davidson, Box 1, Site 8, SS #1, St. Stephen, New Brunswick E3L 2Y4. 506-466-3325. Mohannes, north of St. Stephen. One lodge, one camp, ten guests, mixed groups, showers, indoor plumbing, electricity, guides, boats.

Nepisiguit River Camps, Kenneth Gray, Box 345, RR #5, Bathurst, New Brunswick E2A 3Y8. 506-546-5873. Bathurst area, Nepisiguit River. 8 km (5 miles) from Bathurst on Route 430. Two camps, ten guests, housekeeping, indoor toilet, showers, running water, electricity, guides, bow hunting a specialty.

Salmon River Lodge Ltd., Monte Farrell, P.O. Box 253, Chipman, New Brunswick E0E 1C0. 506-339-6556. Chipman area, Route 116, 26 km (16 miles) from Chipman, 35 km (22 miles) from Harcourt. One lodge, five cottages, twenty-eight guests, mixed groups, dining room, showers, indoor toilets, electricity, telephone, guides.

Auberge du Summit, Robert Y. LaFrance, 8P-Tiso Park, Edmundston, New Brunswick E3V 3K5. 506-735-7662. Hunting and fishing lodge, shower, flush toilets, mixed groups, guide, boats.

Pro-Guides, Ephrem Michaud, P.O. Box 39, St. Leonard, New Brunswick E0L 1M0. 506-423-6689. Route 17, Exit 58 off Route 2. One lodge, cabins, sixteen guests, mixed groups, showers, flush toilets, two boats, guide.

Northumberland County

Cains River Enterprises, Ltd., R. W. W. Brown, 775 Hillsborough Road, Riverview, New Brunswick. 506-386-3604, November 1–April 14; Upper Blackville, New Brunswick. 506-843-6301, April 15–October 31. Cains River, Upper Blackville, off Route 8. Three camps, two lodges, twenty-seven guests, mixed groups, housekeeping, bedding rental only, shower, indoor-outdoor toilets, propane gas, guides, boat rentals.

Campbell's Fishing Camps, Mary Arbeau (manager), RR #1, Upper Blackville, New Brunswick E0C 2C0. 506-843-2586. Off Route 8, 11 km (7 miles) from Blackville on the Howard Road. Seven cottages, twenty-four guests, mixed groups, dining room, showers, indoor toilets, electricity, telephone, guides, canoes. Can arrange canoe trips. Sauna and recreation building with screened porch overlooking trout pond.

Curtis Fishing Camps, John D. Curtis, RR #1, Upper Blackville, New Brunswick. 506-843-2569. 5 km (3 miles) from Blackville on the Howard Road. Two cottages, eight guests, mixed groups, housekeeping, dining room, showers, indoor toilets, electricity, telephone, guides, bow hunting.

Deep Wood Lodge and Big Hole Brook, Dead River Limited, P.O. Box 205, Fredericton, New Brunswick E3B 4Y9. 506-458-8490/365-7890 (Doaktown). Guests are met on arrangement. One lodge, one day lodge, one cabin, eight guests, mixed groups, dining room, showers, indoor toilets, electricity, guides.

Four Men Lodge of N.B. Ltd., John Hanson, Box 310, Fredericton, New Brunswick, 506-836-7755 (Red Bank). Route 425. One lodge, three cottages, ten guests, mixed groups, dining room, showers, indoor toilets, electricity, telephone, guides, boats and motors.

Highbridge Camps, Mirco Limited, Box 100, Newcastle, New Brunswick E1V 3M2. 506-622-0722/836-2846. Sunny Center area, off Route 425. One lodge, one cottage, six guests, mixed groups, housekeeping, dining room, showers, indoor toilets, electricity, telephone, guides, boats, motors, kennels.

Hudson Brook Fishing Club, Richard Underhill (manager), Blackville, New Brunswick E0C 1C0. 506-843-6510/843-2802. Route 118, 1.6 km (1 mile) below Blackville. One lodge, three cottages, sixteen guests, mixed groups, dining room, complete indoor bathrooms, electricity, telephone, guides, boats and motors.

Kelly Lodge, Lloyd Betts, Doaktown, New Brunswick E0C 1G0. 506-365-7602. Hunting and fishing lodge and cabins, bath, shower, flush toilets, mixed groups, guide.

L & W Fishing & Hunting Lodge, Winston J. Curtis, P.O. Box 47, Blackville, New Brunswick E0C 1C0. Route 8. Lodge, bath and shower, flush toilets, mixed groups, guide.

The Lyons Den, Calvin O. Lyons, Doaktown, New Brunswick E0C 1G0. 506-365-4619. 1.6 km (1 mile) off Route 8 on South Road. Three cottages, twelve guests, mixed groups, housekeeping, shower in one, indoor and outdoor toilets, electricity, telephone, guides, one boat.

Mic Mac Salmon Club, Clive W. Wishart, P.O. Box 43, Tabusintac, New Brunswick E0C 2A0. 506-779-9250. Route 11. One lodge, twelve guests, mixed groups, dining room, showers, indoor toilets, electricity, guides, boats and motors.

Millet's On The Cains, Millet Underhill, Blackville, New Brunswick E0C 1C0. 506-843-2869. Off Route 8. Two camps, eight to ten guests, electricity, canoe trips from May 15 to July 20.

Miramichi Inn, (Little Sou'west Farms, Inc.), Andre Godin, RR #2, Red Bank, New Brunswick E0C 1W0. 506-836-7452. Route 108, Halcomb; Route 420, access. One lodge, cabins, six guests, mixed groups, flush toilets, bath, showers, boats, guide.

Miramichi Lodge, Tourchasse Tourpeche Inc., Gilbert Lemay, C.P. 462, Lac St. Charles, Province of Quebec G0A 2H0. 506-849-5134. Blackville, New Brunswick. Routes 8 and 108. Two camps, twelve guests, mixed groups, showers, inside toilets, electricity, propane, boats, guides, bow hunting.

Miramichi Salmon Club, Floyd Gaston (manager), Doaktown, New Brunswick E0C 1G0. 506-365-2289. Route 8. Lodge, bath, shower, flush toilets, seven units, mixed groups, guide, six boats.

Old Mill Boat & Gun Club, Eugene Gillis, Red Bank, New Brunswick E0C 1W0. 506-836-7759/836-7818. Route 420, 1.6 km (1 mile) below Red Bank Bridge. One lodge, three large cottages, two apartments, twenty guests, mixed groups, five housekeeping units, complete indoor bathrooms, electricity, telephone, guides, boats and motors.

Old River Lodge, Ltd., Alex Mills, RR #2, Doaktown, New Brunswick E0G 1G0. 506-365-2253. Route 8. Lodge, cabins, sixteen units, bath, showers, flush toilets, mixed groups, guides, boats.

Pond's (Porter Kove) Kamps, Mrs. Charles (Dodie) Pond, P.O. Box 8, Ludlow, New Brunswick E0C 1N0. 506-369-2228. Route 8, across from Ludlow Bridge. One lodge, four cottages, one to fourteen guests (mixed groups), dining room, showers, indoor toilets, electricity, telephone, guides, canoes, rental equipment, boats and motors.

River Side Guest Home, Thomas Sturgeon, Doaktown, New Brunswick E0C 1G0. 506-365-4685. Route 8 in village of Doaktown. Three cottages, seven guests, mixed groups, showers, indoor toilets, electricity, guides.

Wade's Fishing Lodge, Herbert Wade, 143 Main Street, Fredericton, New Brunswick. 506-843-2288, April 1–October 15/506-472-6454, October 16–March 31. Blackville, Route 8 to Blackville, cross S.W. Miramichi River on Route 118, proceed south 13 km (8 miles) to across river from Howard. One lodge, three cottages, nineteen guests, mixed groups, dining room, showers, indoor toilets, electricity, telephone, guides, canoes.

Wilson's Sporting Camps Ltd., Keith Wilson, McNamee, New Brunswick E0C 1P0. 506-365-7962. 3 km (2 miles) off Route 8 at McNamee. One lodge, eight camps, two outpost camps (2 housekeeping); twenty-five guests, mixed groups, dining room, baths and showers, indoor toilets, electricity, telephone, guides, canoes, bow hunting.

Wishart's Hunting & Fishing Camps, Myles Wishart, Box 124, Wishart's Point, RR #2, Tabusintac, New Brunswick E0C 2A0. 506-779-9230. Route 11. One lodge, ten guests, mixed groups, dining room, complete indoor bathrooms, electricity, telephone, guides, boats and motors, kennels.

Queens County

Eagle's Rest, 9 Myles Drive, Saint John, New Brunswick E2J 3E1. 506-696-1273. Belyea's Cove between Wickham and Shannon, Queens County Route 710 off 2 and 705. One lodge, four units, mixed groups, guide, boats.

Gerald's Place, Gerald C. Sarchfield, RR #1, Cody's, New Brunswick E0E 1E0. 506-362-2974/488-2737. Cambridge Narrows, Cody's on Washademoak Lake. Route 710. Lodge, three bunkhouses, bunkbeds, twenty-six guests, mixed groups, new washroom building, showers and indoor toilets, guide, boats.

Hector View Camp, Wayne W. Black, Coles Island, New Brunswick E0E 1G0. 506-534-2985. Route 112 off old Fredericton Road near Hector Brook. Lodge, dry toilet, mixed groups, guide, boats.

McIntyre's Motor Motel and Restaurant, Derwyn McIntyre, Waterborough, New Brunswick E0E 1S0. 506-362-2913. Route 2. Summer: thirteen cabins available, motel, forty-five guests, mixed groups, restaurant and liquor-licensed dining room, complete indoor bathrooms, electricity, telephones, guides, bow hunting. Take-out and room service. Swimming.

Hotel Kedgwick, Gilles Girrard, C.P. 237, St. Jean Baptiste, Kedgwick, New Brunswick E0K 1C0. 506-284-2638. St. Jean Baptiste, Route 17. Hotel, five units, restaurant, bath, shower.

Victoria County

Bodell Lodge, Harold Demerchant, P.O. Box 336, Perth Andover, New Brunswick E0J 1V0. 506-273-2187. Route 109. Hunting and fishing lodge, flush toilets, shower, hot and cold water, six persons, mixed groups, guide.

Black's Hunting and Fishing Camps, Juanita Black, RR #1, Plaster Rock, New Brunswick E0J 1W0. 506-356-2429. Nictau, Route 385, 48 km (30 miles) north of Plaster Rock. Two camps, two lodges, six cottages, thirty guests, mixed groups, dining room, showers, indoor toilets, electricity, telephone, guides, canoes, one dog for hunting, kennels.

Black Mountain Camps, John A. MacKellar, Arthurette, New Brunswick E0J 1C0. 506-273-3738. Arthurette area, Route 109, 24 km (15 miles) southeast of Arthurette. Two lodges, twelve guests, mixed groups, dining room, indoor toilets, hot water, guides.

C. H. Hunting Camp, Collins E. Hudnut, RR #2, Plaster Rock, New Brunswick E0J 1W0. 506-356-2097. 5 miles west of Plaster Rock on Route 108. One lodge, five guests, mixed groups, showers, bath, flush toilets, guide, boats.

Chicamoor Lodge, Paul Williams, 489 Island Road, Lunenburg, MA 01462. 617-582-4868. Route 109. One lodge, ten guests, mixed groups, housekeeping, showers, indoor toilets, electricity, guides.

Dyer's Hunting and Fishing Camps, Lawrence A. Dyer, Box 216, Plaster Rock, New Brunswick E0J 1W0. 506-356-2292/356-2854. 11 km (7 miles) east of Plaster Rock on

Route 108. One lodge, three cottages, thirty-eight guests, mixed groups, dining room, showers, indoor toilets, electricity, telephone, shortwave radio, guides, three boats and motors, canoes, kennels, bow hunting. Ten guests in outcamp in woods 20 miles from Plaster Rock on Wapske River.

Hanson's Lodge, Murray Hanson, Box 877, RR #5, Perth Andover, New Brunswick E0J 1V0. 506-273-2844. Route 109. Hunting and fishing lodge and cabins, bath, shower, flush toilets, eight persons, mixed groups, guide, boats.

Howard's Camp, Ralph and Gladys Howard, RR #1, Riley Brook, New Brunswick E0J 1W0. 506-356-2481. Route 385. One lodge, eight guests, mixed groups, dining room, showers, indoor toilets, electricity, telephone, canoe, guides, rifle and bow hunting, home cooking.

Joe's Place, Joe Williams, 57 Round Road, Lunenburg, MA 01462. 617-582-7707. Summit, Plaster Rock, Route 107. One lodge, six guests, mixed groups, housekeeping, shower, indoor toilet, propane gas, guides.

Little Bald Peak Lodge, Allison King, RR #1, Plaster Rock, New Brunswick E0J 1W0. 506-356-2354. Route 385. Three lodges (one lodge, housekeeping, off season), nineteen guests, mixed groups, dining room, baths and showers, indoor toilets, electricity, telephone, guides, canoes, kennels, bow hunting.

Mamozekel Lodge, Robert Miller, RR #1, Plaster Rock, New Brunswick E0J 1W0. 506-356-2256. Nictau area, 13 km (8 miles) north of Nictau on Route 385. Two lodges, eight guests, mixed groups, dining room, showers, indoor toilets, propane gas, fridge, guides, canoes, kennels, bow hunting.

Melvin's Hunting-Fishing Lodge, Melvin B. Sirois, P.O. Box 481, Plaster Rock, New Brunswick E0J 1W0. 506-473-1859. Longley Siding, Plaster Rock. Hunting and fishing lodge.

Mountain Spring Lodge, Mildred Yeomans, RR #2, Plaster Rock, New Brunswick E0J 1W0. 506-356-8848. RR #2, Plaster Rock, off 2 on 108. One lodge, bath and shower, mixed groups, guide.

McQuade's Camp, Stillman McQuade, RR #1, Plaster Rock, New Brunswick E0J 1W0. 506-356-2780. 3 Riley Brook, Route 385. One lodge, ten guests, mixed groups, housekeeping, showers, indoor toilets, propane gas, telephone, boat.

Neilson's Sporting Camps, Neil G. Neilson, Plaster Rock, New Brunswick E0J 1W0. 506-356-2391. Plaster Rock area, Route 109. Guests are met. Two camps, fourteen guests, men only, dining room, outdoor toilets, guides, motor canoes.

Northern Wilderness Lodge, Gerald Shaw, Box 385, Plaster Rock, New Brunswick E0J 1W0. 506-356-8327. Tobique River, 8 km (5 miles) south from Plaster Rock on Route 390 at intersection of Route 380. One lodge, twenty-four guests, mixed groups, dining room, baths and showers, indoor toilets, electricity, telephone, C.B. radio, guides, canoes, kennels, bow hunting.

Nictau Lodge, Fred A. Webb, RR #1, Plaster Rock, New Brunswick E0J 1W0. 506-356-8312. 48 km (30 miles) north of Plaster Rock on Route 385. Two camps, two lodges, three cottages, fifty guests, mixed groups, dining room, housekeeping, showers, indoor toilets, telephone, electricity, guides, canoes.

Odell Lodge, Jean Louis Page, Box 18, Park Street, Grand Falls, New Brunswick E0J 1M0. 506-473-3263. Plaster Rock, off 2 on 109. One lodge, six beds, shower, flush toilets, mixed groups, guide boats.

Riley Brook Camps, Ltd., Stephen F. and Ivan N. McAskill, RR #1, Plaster Rock, New Brunswick E0J 1W0. 506-356-2005/356-2315. Route 385. Four cottages, fifteen guests, mixed groups, dining room, showers, indoor toilets, electricity, telephone, guides, boat and motor, bow hunting.

River View Camp, Donald McAskill, RR #1, Plaster Rock, New Brunswick E0J 1W0. 506-356-8351. Route 385. Lodge, six guests, mixed groups, shower, flush toilet, guides, boats and motors.

Romeo's Maple Lodge, Romeo Rossingol, RR #2, New Denmark, New Brunswick E0J 1T0. 506-356-2239. Annderson Road, New Denmark, off Route 2 on 380. One lodge, shower, flush toilets, ten guests, mixed groups, guide, boats, sugar bush camp, sleigh rides, fish pond, home cooked meals, hay rides, X-C skiing.

Ruff's Sporting Camps, Edward Ruff/John Ruff, RR #1, Plaster Rock, New Brunswick E0J 1W0. Eight miles north of Plaster Rock, Route 385. One lodge, one camp, fifteen guests, mixed groups, showers, flush toilets, guide, boat.

Sutherland Hunting Camp, William Sutherland, RR #1, Plaster Rock, New Brunswick E0J 1W0. 506-356-2467. Woods camp north of Nictau, Route 385. Lodge, two camps, ten guests, mixed groups, showers, flush toilets, guide, boats, bow hunting.

The Lucky 7 Camp, David E. Parish, RR #1, Plaster Rock, New Brunswick E0J 1W0. 506-356-8311. Riley Brook area, Route 385. One lodge, eight guests, mixed groups, dining room, showers, indoor toilets, electricity, guides, boats and motors, bow hunting.

Tobique Lodge, Ursula Schmidt, RR #1, Plaster Rock, New Brunswick E0J 1W0. 506-356-8366. Riley Brook, Route 385. Lodge, three units, flush toilets, mixed groups, guide.

Tobique River Lodge, Jim and Lena Lacey, RR #1, Plaster Rock, New Brunswick E0J 1W0. 506-356-2000. Ox Bow, Route 385, 12 miles from Plaster Rock, Route 108 from Grand Falls, Route 109 from Perth Andover. One lodge, seven guests, flush toilets, bath, showers, guide, boats.

Tobique & Serpentine, Lewis and Edythe McAskill, RR #1, Plaster Rock, New Brunswick E0J 1W0. 506-356-2215. Tobique Camps at Riley Brook on Route 385. Three camps, fifteen hunters per week. Serpentine camps 22 miles in wilderness, six hunters per week. Showers, flush toilets, basins, dining room, propane gas, electricity, telephone, boats and motors, canoes, guides, rifle and bow hunting.

Tobique View Motel & Sporting Camps, William Linton, P.O. Box 571, Plaster Rock, New Brunswick E0J 1W0. 506-356-2441. Route 108 near Plaster Rock. Restaurant, lounge, five housekeeping units, one log cabin, twelve motel units, all equipped with telephone, showers, and color TV.

The Renaissance Registered, Erma Knowlton, Box 35, Main Street, Plaster Rock, New Brunswick E0J 1W0. 506-356-8821. Route 108, Route 2 Exits 75 and 115. Twelve units, twenty-four guests, mixed groups, dining room, complete indoor bathrooms, electricity, telephone, guides.

Windy Hill Lodge, Albert Scafordi, Riley Brook, New Brunswick. Route 385. One lodge, eight guests, mixed groups, dining room, showers, indoor toilets, electricity, guide.

York County

Condor Lodge, Ider and Kamal Bedi, P.O. Box 801, Woodstock Road, Fredericton, New Brunswick E3B 5B4. 506-455-5537. Fredericton area, junction Routes 2 and 102, 5 km from city center, 15 km from Lake Mactaquac. One lodge, fifty units, fully equipped (indoor pool, games room, color TV), licensed dining room, guides, boats and motors available, special group rates on request.

MacFarlan's Sporting Camps, Dixon MacFarlan, Millville, New Brunswick E0H 1M0. 506-463-8102. Hawkins Corner, junction 104 and 585. Hunting and fishing lodge, bath and shower, flush toilets, guide, boats.

Shogomoc Camps, Willard Way, RR #3, Nackawic, New Brunswick E0H 1P0. 506-272-2171. Charlie Lake, off Route 2, 8 km (5 miles) above Pokiok; follow the signs. One lodge, four cottages (one housekeeping); twelve guests, mixed groups, dining room, fridge, showers, indoor toilets, electricity, telephone, guides, boats and canoes, outboard motor, bow hunting.

Sunset Park Fishing, Albert R. Barton, RR #3 (Hawkshaw), Nackawic, New Brunswick. 506-472-7811/575-2592. Near Nackawic, off Route 2 (Trans-Canada), Hawkshaw 27 km west of Kings Landing. Cottages, six guests, mixed groups, showers, bath, flush toilets.

Sunset View Lodge, Jack H. Grant (manager), RR #1, McAdam, New Brunswick E0H 1K0. 506-784-2928. McAdam area, 8 km (5 miles) on Route 630 from Route 4. Lodge, cabins, fourteen guests, mixed groups, showers, flush toilets, guide, boats.

Thornton's Sporting Camps, Beatrice S. Thornton, P.O. Box 452, Hartland, New Brunswick E0J 1N0. 506-375-6632. Temperance Vale, take Route 605 at Nackawic, Exit 232 to Route 595 at Temperance Vale, then 2½ miles up Pike Hill. Hunting lodge, shower, flush toilets, two couples, guide.

PRINCE EDWARD ISLAND

Licenses and Fees: Trout angling licenses can be obtained from authorized vendors around the province and at the Fish and Wildlife Division Office, 3 Queen Street, Charlottetown.

Salmon licenses are available only at the Fish and Wildlife Office, from Conservation officers, or from Federal Fishery offices and officers. *Please note:* The trout licenses (resident and non-resident) will entitle the licensee to angle brook and rainbow trout only.

An Atlantic salmon angling license is required, in addition to a trout license, to angle Atlantic salmon.

Resident Trout Angling License . . . . $ 5.00
Courtesy Resident Trout Angling License (65 years of age and over) . . . . free
Non-Resident Trout Angling License (family members may angle for a
    period of 2 weeks from date of issue) $12.00

Atlantic Salmon Angling License (must also possess Trout Angling
   License if required) .... $ 5.00

Atlantic Salmon:

Daily limit of 1. Possession limit of 1.
Season limit of 5. (Five tags supplied with each license.)
All salmon longer than 63 cm (25 inches) must be released immediately with the least
possible harm to the fish.
Open season July 1 to September 30.
Hook and release only, October 1–31.
All salmon must be tagged upon capture.
No person shall angle salmon except by fly fishing.
No person shall fish for, kill, or retain any spent or slink salmon.
Atlantic salmon fishing on Prince Edward Island is done mostly in the Morell River.
Open season is July 1–September 30, with a catch limit of one a day and a season limit
of five; all must be tagged. A special license is required for fishing salmon. Most
Atlantic salmon weigh between 2 and 5 kg (4½ to 11 pounds), although anglers are
allowed to keep grilse only.

NEWFOUNDLAND/LABRADOR

Season Dates: Three sets of opening/closing dates have been set for *most* rivers in three
respective areas of the island portion of the province.

	Open	Close
Cape Ray, north to and including Bonne Bay	June 7	September 1
Cape Bauld to Cape Ray (east and south coasts)	June 14	September 7
North of Bonne Bay to Cape Bauld	June 21	September 1

The following rivers are exceptions within these areas:

	Open	Close
Northwest Brook, Grand Bay	June 1	September 1
Bear Cove River	June 1	September 1
St. Genevieve River: Ten-Mile Lake and Round Lake and tributary streams	June 1	September 1
Conne River	June 7	September 1
Garnish River	June 7	September 1
Upper Humber River (Deer Lake to Big Falls; the dates for all other sections of the Humber, June 7–September 1)	June 7	September 14

Southeast River, Placentia	June 21	September 1
Northeast River, Placentia	June 21	September 1
Indian River	June 21	September 1
Exploits River	June 21	September 1
Terra Nova River	June 21	September 1
Little Salmonier River	June 21	September 1
West River, St. Barbe	June 21	September 1
Fox Island River	June 21	September 1
Watson's Brook	June 21	September 1
Little Codroy River	June 28	September 1
Harry's River	June 28	September 1
Little Barachois River	June 28	September 1

Torrent River and tributaries will be opened when it has been determined that 1,000 salmon have passed upstream through the fishway; an announcement will be made at the approximate time. This river will close September 1, 1987.

Labrador:	Open	Close
Pinware River	June 7	September 14
Forteau River	June 7	September 14
Lanse au Loup River	June 7	September 14
All other rivers	June 14	September 14

Bag Limits: New bag limit regulations for salmon have been introduced this year in Newfoundland and Labrador. The major changes are the introduction of: (1) a *daily* limit of four on the number of fish that may be hooked and released, and (2) a *season* limit of fifteen on the number of fish that may be retained. Salmon anglers should read the following points carefully; anyone needing further information or clarification should contact the Department of Fisheries and Oceans.

The daily limit for salmon retained is two.

The daily limit for salmon hooked and released is four.

When one or the other of these limits has been reached, the angler must cease fishing for the day.

The season limit for salmon retained is fifteen; when this limit has been reached the angler must cease fishing for the season.

On the island of Newfoundland, grilse only may be retained. For the purpose of these regulations, a grilse shall be a salmon measuring between 30 cm (12 inches) and 63 cm (24.8 inches) from the tip of the nose to the fork of the tail.

In Labrador, anglers may retain large salmon (fish measuring 63 cm or more in length) as well as grilse.

Tagging Requirements: The provinces of Quebec, Nova Scotia, New Brunswick, and Prince Edward Island require that any Atlantic salmon transported within their borders must bear a recognized salmon tag. To comply with these regulations, anglers wishing to bring salmon into these provinces may obtain Newfoundland export tags from local DFO fishery officers or from the area offices in St. John's, Grand Bank, Grand Falls, and Corner Brook, or the Goose Bay district office.

Licensed Guide Requirements: Every non-resident licensed to fish for salmon may fish within 400 meters (one-quarter mile) upstream and 400 meters downstream of any bridge or any highway of the province crossing any scheduled river, without employing and being accompanied by a licensed guide. In all other situations, licensed guides must be employed. One guide is required for each two non-resident fishermen.

License Fees:

	Standard License	Family License*
Salmon		
resident, season	$10.00	$15.00
non-resident, season +	$40.00	$60.00
Trout		
non-resident	$10.00	$15.00

*Includes children 17 and under.
+ Non-resident salmon licenses may also be used to fish all.

Hunting and Fishing Guide: For further information on recreational fishing (and hunting) in Newfoundland and Labrador—including detailed information on individual salmon rivers, licensed guides and outfitters, and many other items of interest—consult *Newfoundland and Labrador Hunting and Fishing*. This booklet is published by the Tourism Branch, Department of Development and Tourism, P.O. Box 2016, St. John's, Newfoundland A1C 5T7 (phone 576-2802), and is available free at tourist information chalets, and Department of Fisheries and Oceans offices throughout the province (Newfoundland Region, P.O. Box 5667, St. John's, Newfoundland A1C 5X1, 709-772-4421; Gulf Region, Newfoundland/Labrador, P.O. Box 2099, Corner Brook, Newfoundland A2H 6Z6, 709-637-4320).

Outfitters:

Brophy and Sons Outfitting, Steadman Brophy, P.O. Box 33, Daniel's Harbour, Newfoundland. 709-898-2557. Brophy can accommodate six anglers at his fishing camp on

Leslie Lake for speckled trout and access to salmon on the Main River. Accessible by float plane.

Chignic Lodge and Cabins, Doyles, Newfoundland A0N 1J0. 709-955-2880/2881. Provides accommodations in eight housekeeping cabins and twelve motel units located in the Trans-Canada Highway about 50 km from Port aux Basques. Chignic cabins lie adjacent to the Codroy River. Local guides may be arranged.

James and Lorraine Gillam, South Branch, Newfoundland A0N 2B0. 709-955-2433. Operate a cabin at South Branch within easy driving distance of the Codroy River. Fishing parties accommodated.

Hammond Outfitters, Leo Hammond, Box 53, Doyles, Newfoundland A0N 1J0. 709-955-2417. Offers daily, three-day, or weekly fishing packages on the Codroy, North Branch, and South Branch River systems with accommodations in local house-keeping units. Local guides and home cooked meals provided. Fishing packages tailored to the angler's requirements.

Hare Brothers Outfitters, P.O. Box 492, Burgeo, Newfoundland A0M 1A0. 709-886-2805. Operates a lodge with accommodations for six guests, which consists of three double bedrooms. Excellent food service. Information available upon request.

Woodland Lodge Limited, Don McInnis, Highlands, Newfoundland A0N 1N0. 709-639-7309. Can accommodate four salmon anglers at his Mitchell Pond cabin, offering fishing at Robinsons, Crabbes, Fishells, Barachois, Flat Bay, and the Codroy rivers. Meals, guides, and transportation included.

Mountainview Motel, Box 15, Daniel's Harbour, Newfoundland A0K 2C0. 709-898-2211. Offers daily, weekend, or weekly fishing packages that include accommodations, meals, and guides. Fish for Atlantic salmon, speckled trout, or sea run trout at Port-land Creek and nearby areas. For rates please contact Leonard Payne, Manager.

William A. Ryan, RR #1, P.O. Box 176, O'Regans, Newfoundland. 709-955-2835. Operates Island View Cabin on the banks of the Grand Codroy River. The main lodge accommodates four anglers; separate cookhouse and dining area. Excellent salmon angling in this area.

Heatherton Lodge, Alan and Ed Skinner, P.O. Box 615, Stephenville, Newfoundland A2N 3B4. Can accommodate four people per week, and from there you can fish

Robinsons, Fischells, and Middle Barachoix River. There is good trout fishing minutes away by road. Hiking and canoeing trips can also be arranged. Guests are asked to supply their own rain gear and sleeping bags.

Viking Trail Salmon Outfitters, c/o Maynard's Motor Inn, Hawke's Bay, Newfoundland A0K 3B0. 709-248-5225. Provides accommodations in twenty motel units, six efficiency units, and six housekeeping units. Weekly or weekend packages include transportation to and from Deer Lake Airport, guides, accommodations, and excellent dining facilities. Fishing is provided for Atlantic salmon and speckled trout at several sites and rivers within easy driving distance. Remote fly-in trips arranged on request. For further information and rates contact Bill Maynard.

Deer Pond Camps, Angus N. Wentzell, P.O. Box 9, Corner Brook, Newfoundland A2H 6C3. 709-634-2347. Can accommodate six anglers at each of his camps on Angus Lake and Four Ponds in the Main River area with fine salmon and trout fishing. Camps reached by float plane from Pasadena.

Rendell C. Wentzell, River of Ponds, Newfoundland. 709-225-3551. Maintains five fishing cabins for daily rental at River of Ponds.

James Hefford, 33 Poplar Road, Corner Brook, Newfoundland A2H 4T6. 709-634-7544. Can accommodate four sports fishermen at his establishment at Howley, which has modern conveniences and ready access by road to several salmon streams. Located on the shore of Sandy Lake. Trout fishing readily available.

Swift Current, Placentia Bay, Edwin Beck, Newfoundland A0E 2W0. 709-549-2225. Operates Brookside Cabins near Swift Current with access to salmon angling at Piper's Hole River.

David Brown, P.O. Box 1028, Clarenville, Newfoundland A0E 1J0. 709-466-2986/3045. Operates a modern lodge for salmon anglers at Meta Pond on the headwaters of Long Harbour River.

Buchaneer Outback Ltd., P.O. Box 118, Buchans, Newfoundland A2A 2J3. 709-489-4000. Operates the Owl's Nest Lodge on Hinds Lake in the Buchans area. Angling offered for speckled trout and ouananiche on Hinds Lake and other nearby lakes. Daily salmon angling trips on the Exploits River in season. Family groups accommodated at the modern three-story "A" frame and cabins. Group rates available.

Howard John, P.O. Box 373, St. Albans, Bay D'Espoir, Newfoundland A0H 2E0. 709-538-3411. Operates John's Hunting and Fishing Lodge on the Conne River about 5 km off Route 360 to Bay D'Espoir with excellent speckled trout and salmon angling in the early run stream. The lodge has all modern conveniences with meals and guides included in the package.

Bill Lynch, P.O. Box 556, Grand Falls, Newfoundland A2A 2S9. 709-489-4662. Can accommodate four anglers at his modern cabin on Sandy Lake near Badger, a tributary of the Exploits River. The cabin contains all conveniences.

Donald G. Penny, P.O. Box 5188, St. John's, Newfoundland A1C 5V5. 709-726-0777. Operates Grey River Lodge at the Grey River just below Smokey Falls, accessible only by helicopter. The lodge contains all modern conveniences and can accommodate six guests. Package includes helicopter transport, food, lodging, and guides. Salmon fishing only.

Calvin Saunders, P.O. Box 353, Gander, Newfoundland. 709-256-8466. Operates Minnehaha Hunting and Fishing Service to accommodate ten guests at his lodge on First Pond, Gander River, with all modern conveniences, home cooked meals, guides, and boat and motors. The lodge is accessible by river boat or float plane from Gander. Salmon angling.

Dave Toms, P.O. Box 361, Bishop's Falls, Newfoundland. 709-258-6210. Offers fishing for speckled trout and Atlantic salmon from his Beaver Mountain Lodge on Great Rattling Brook, a part of the Exploits River, with accommodations for six anglers.

Double Mer Fish Camp Limited, P.O. Box 77, Station B, Happy Valley, Labrador. 709-896-2635. Double Mer Lake. A modern log cabin fishing lodge is operated by Howard Michelin at the inlet to Double Mer Lake, where speckled trout, arctic char, and Atlantic salmon may be caught in the tidal pools or further upriver.

Forteau Salmon Lodge, L'Anse au Clair, Labrador A0K 3K0. 709-931-2332. Forteau River. Accessible by road and a short ferry ride across the Strait of Belle Isle from St. Barbe, the Forteau River lies in the southeast corner of Labrador. Steve and Shirley Letto operate Forteau Salmon Lodge with indoor plumbing, home cooked meals, local guides, and comfortable accommodations for up to fourteen anglers. River boats assure access to all salmon pools. Atlantic salmon and speckled trout fishing excellent from early July onward.

Gander Aviation Limited, P.O. Box 250, Gander, Newfoundland A1V 1W6. 709-256-3421. Michael's River. A modern lodge with two suites, four double bedrooms, excellent food service, and experienced guides is operated on the Michael's River by W. J. (Bill) Bennett. Atlantic salmon, arctic char, and speckled trout may be caught here. Parties of up to twelve guests accommodated. Air transportation from Goose Bay included.

Sandhill River. Accommodations for six guests in three double bedrooms, indoor plumbing, and home cooked meals are provided on the Sandhill River by W. J. (Bill) Bennett. The Sandhill lies on the Labrador coast east of Goose Bay and offers excellent Atlantic salmon and trout fishing. Air transportation from Goose Bay included in package. Brochures, maps, recommended dates for angling salmon and trout at Michael's River and Sandhill River are available on request.

Goose Bay Outfitters Limited, c/o Peter P. Paor, 5 Lomac Road, St. John's, Newfoundland A1A 3M8, 709-753-0550 (winter); Box 171, Station B, Happy Valley, Labrador A0P 1E0, 709-896-2423 (summer). Adlatok River. Peter and Alma Paor provide accommodations for four anglers on the Adlatok River some 200 km north of Goose Bay. The lodge has two double-occupancy cabins and a main dining/living cabin with all modern conveniences and home cooked meals. A large run of grilse and salmon with minimal angling pressure assures good fishing.

Lower Eagle River Salmon Lodge. Up to twelve anglers may be accommodated in six double-occupancy cabins at the Lower Eagle River Lodge operated by Peter and Alma Paor. The main lodge contains hot and cold running water, home cooked meals, and all modern conveniences. The lodge lies near the gorge at picturesque Eagle Falls, the mouth of this 240-km river. Atlantic salmon fishing at its best from mid-July to mid-September.

Hunt River Outfitters, P.O. Box 307, Goose Bay, Labrador A0P 1S0. 709-896-8049. Hunt River. A modern lodge and sleeping cabins to accommodate eight anglers is operated at the Hunt River by Clyde House. Inside plumbing, home cooked meals, knowledgeable guides included. The Hunt River lies northeast of Goose Bay and has excellent salmon fishing during July and August.

Klub Kavisilik, c/o Shannon Enterprises Ltd., P.O. Box 104, Vypon Acres, RR #1, Arnprior, Ontario K7S 3G7. 709-623-2659. Flowers River. Jerry Shannon operates Klub Kavisilik, a modern lodge at the mouth of the Flowers River, offering angling for Atlantic salmon and sea run brook trout. Side trips by float plane for arctic char, lake trout, and speckled trout as weather permits. Home cooked meals, modern plumbing, and seasoned guides.

Labrador Sports Fish Limited, Vince Burton, Box 411, Goose Bay, Labrador A0P 1C0. St. John's, 709-364-1001; Goose Bay, 709-896-3901 (summer). Eagle River Lodge. Located about 24 km up the Eagle River, this modern lodge can accommodate six anglers fly fishing for Atlantic salmon and brook trout. Salmon are caught on the flats just upriver from Eagle Lodge. Guides, meals, and comfortable rooms included in this package.

Flowers River Lodge. Located about 275 km north of Goose Bay, the Flowers River has excellent Atlantic salmon, arctic char, and sea run trout from late July to mid-September. Vince Burton operates a modern panabode log lodge to accommodate eight guests with all comforts and conveniences. Float plane available for side trips to more remote sites on request.

Lakeland Lodge, P.O. Box 250, Pasadena, Newfoundland A0L 1K0. 709-686-2242. Big River. A modern log lodge is operated by Bob Skinner at Big River, about 200 km northeast of Goose Bay, with accommodations for up to fourteen anglers. Modern bathroom facilities, home cooked meals, seasoned guides, boats and motors, and refrigeration included. Big River has excellent runs of Atlantic salmon and sea run trout from early July to the end of August.

Lucky Strike Lodge, Hedley Normore, P.O. Box 73, L'Anse au Loup, Labrador A0K 3L0. 709-927-5657/927-5648. Pinware River. Can accommodate fourteen fishermen on the Pinware River. Meals, boats, and guides are provided at this modern establishment, situated only minutes away from the most popular pools.

Pinware River Lodge, 21 W. Elm Street, Chicago, IL 60610. 312-642-4550. (Or call for information: Arthur Fowler, 709-925-5785, L'Anse au Loup, Labrador, Newfoundland A0K 3L0.) Overlooking the Pinware River at the spectacular bridge site, the newly remodeled Pinware River Lodge offers luxurious accommodations and personalized service for six to eight fishermen in a classic river lodge. The lodge is located within easy access to all the salmon pools. In addition, the staff and guides are eager to provide a total Labrador experience and can arrange trout fishing, craft shop forays, and visits to local tourist sites.

Powell's Outfitters, Charlottetown, Labrador A0K 5Y0. 709-949-0040. Gilbert River. The Gilbert River lies along the southeast coast of Labrador and is accessible by float plane or boat. Tony Powell operates a modern and comfortable lodge at the river mouth with accommodations for ten anglers. Excellent Atlantic salmon, arctic char, sea run and speckled trout fishing. Side trips to nearby rivers by boat. Float plane based at camp for daily trips to interior lakes, weather permitting.

QUEBEC
Outfitters Offering Atlantic Salmon Fishing:

Pourvoirie le Chasseur Inc., 1900 Boul. Gaboury, C.P. 248, Mont-Joli, Quebec G5H 3L1. 418-775-3655. Kedgwick River, Route 298, to Saint-Charles-Garnier and bush road to the outfitter. Rowboat, launch, ramp, freezer, ice dispenser, electricity, services of a guide.

Helen McWhirter-Campbell, C.P. 37, Grande-Cascapedia, Quebec G0C 1T0. 418-392-6148. Little Cascapedia River. Route 132 to New Richmond and the old road to St.-Edgar (10 km). Canoes, launch ramp, life jacket, freezer, washers, dryers, ice dispensers, electricity, services of a guide.

Le Club de Saumon Saint-Jean de Gaspé, 35 Barat Road, Montreal, Quebec H3Y 2H3. 514-935-9648/418-368-2603. St.-Jean River. Route 198 from Gaspé to Sunny Rank and bush road to the outfitter. Fishing tackle, canoes.

Pourvoirie Etamamiou, 20 rue Marquette, Baie-Comeau, Quebec G4K 1K6. 418-296-7643/296-7471. Gagnon Lake, Route 138 to Havre-St. Pierre and by plane. Fishing tackle, rowboat, motors, launch ramp, life jacket, freezer, ice dispenser, electricity, services of a guide.

Pourvoirie R. Geoffroy, Inc., C.P. 969, New-Richmond, Quebec G0C 2B0. 418-534-2230/392-5168. Nabissipi River, Route 138 to Havre-St. Pierre and by plane. Rowboat, motors, life jacket, ice dispensers, electricity, services of a guide.

Brigitte et Elmar Engel, La Tabatiere, Quebec G0G 1T0. 418-773-2354. Kecarpoui River, by plane to St. Augustin and by boat (32 km) to the outfitter. Rowboat, electricity.

Samuel S. Fequet, Old Fort Bay, Quebec GOG 2G0. 418-379-2981. Lac du Vieux Fort, Route 138 to Havre-St-Pierre and by plane. Rowboat, motors, launch ramp, life jacket, freezer, ice dispensers, electricity, hunting and fishing licenses, services of a guide.

Leslie Foreman, Kegaska, Quebec G0G 1S0; 1485 Stanley, Montreal, Quebec H3A 1P6. 514-726-3275/726-3385. Kegaska River, by plane via Ste-Anne-des-Monts. Canoes, rowboat, motors, life jacket, freezer, washers, electricity, hunting and fishing licenses, services of a guide.

Club Chasse et Peche Gabou Inc., 921 Godin, Ville-Vanier, Quebec G1M 2X5. 418-681-5449. Achigan Lake, Route 138 to Havre-St-Pierre and by plane. Canoes, rowboat, motors, life jacket, freezer, washers, ice dispensers, electricity, services of a guide.

Pourvoirie Hipu, Bande de Natashquan, Reserve indienne, Pointe-Parent, Quebec. 418-726-3609/726-3529. Pointe Parent, Route 138 to Sept-iles and by plane. Rowboat, motors, launch ramp, life jacket, freezer, washers, electricity, hunting and fishing licenses, services of a guide.

Club de Peche au Saumon Saint-Paul Inc., 1360 des Gouverneurs, Quebec. G1T 2G5. 418-527-4877/688-0691. Saint-Paul River, Route 138 to Havre-St-Pierre and by plane. Fishing tackle, canoes, motors, life jacket, freezer, washers, electricity, services of a guide.

La Loge Mecatina Inc., C.P. 1174, Station B, Hull, Quebec J8X 3X7. 613-728-7599/418-773-2289. Gros Mecatina River, Route 138 to Baie-Comeau and by plane. Canoes, rowboat, motors, life jacket, freezer, washers, electricity, hunting and fishing licenses, services of a guide.

Club de Peche de la Haute-Moisie Inc., 7525 place Martin, Charlesbourg, Quebec G1H 6C7. 418-626-0058. Moisie River, by plane via Sept-iles. Rowboat, motors, life jacket, freezer, ice dispensers, services of a guide.

La Societe des Establissements de Plein Air du Quebec, 1650 Louis Jette, Quebec, Quebec G1S 2W3. 418-535-0156/800-463-0863. Salmon River, Route 138 to Sept-iles and plane to Port-Menier. Pleasure boats, canoes, life jacket, freezer, washers, dryers, ice dispensers, electricity, hunting and fishing licenses, services of a guide.

Pourvoirie du Lac Genevieve, C.P. 69, Port-Menier, Quebec G0G 2Y0. 418-535-0294. Genevieve Lake, Route 138 to Sept-iles and plane to Port-Menier. Fishing tackle, canoes, rowboat, life jacket, freezer, ice dispensers, electricity, services of a guide.

La Pourvoirie du Cerf-Sau Inc., 40 Racine, Loretteville, Quebec G2B 1C6. 418-843-0173/514-655-3652. Chaloupe River, Route 138 to Sept-iles and plane to Port-

Menier. Freezer, washers, dryers, electricity, hunting and fishing licenses, services of a guide.

Les Pourvoiries d'Anticosti Inc., 149 Notre-Dame, C.P. 398, Cap-Chat, Quebec G0J 1E0. 418-786-5788/786-2881. Bell River, Route 138 to Havre-St-Pierre and plane to Port-Menier. Water blinds, trapping devices, life jacket, freezer, washers, dryers, ice dispensers, electricity, hunting and fishing licenses, services of a guide.

Les Pourvoyeurs de la Riviere Corneille, Inc., 1 Place Ville-Marie, Suite 3725, Montreal, Quebec H3B 3P4. 514-878-9641/879-1401/245-7017. Corneille River, Route 138 to Havre-St. Pierre and by plane. Rowboat, motors, ice dispensers, electricity, hunting and fishing licenses, services of a guide.

La Pourvoirie Baie Johan-Beetz Inc., Baie-Johan-Beetz, Quebec G0G 1B0. 418-539-0137. Baie Johan Beetz, Route 138 to Havre-St-Pierre and by plane. Fishing tackle, rowboat, motors, life jacket, washers, dryers, electricity, services of a guide.

La Pourvoirie de la Riviere Washicoutai Ltee, 1245 Sherbrooke ouest, Suite 1600, Montreal, Quebec H3G 1G2. 514-849-1196/879-2334. Washicoutai River, Route 138 to Havre-St-Pierre and by plane. Rowboat, motors, launch ramp, life jacket, washers, ice dispensers, electricity, hunting and fishing licenses, services of a guide.

Pourvoirie de la Haute Saint-Jean Enr., Eiviere St-Jean, Quebec G0G 2N0. 418-949-2210. St-Jean River, helicopter from Sept-iles. Freezer, ice dispensers, electricity, services of a guide.

Pourvoirie Moisie-Quapetec (1986) Inc., C.P. 1645, Sept-iles, Quebec G4R 5C7. 418-968-8449. Moisie River, helicopter from Sept-iles. Ice dispensers, electricity, services of a guide.

Pourvoirie Moisie-Nipissis Inc., B.P. 444, Sept-iles, Quebec G4R 4B6. 418-962-1334. Nipissis River, Route 138 to Sept-iles and by plane. Freezer, ice dispensers, electricity, services of a guide.

Pourvoirie Tonkas Enr., 100 rue Retty, Sept-iles, Quebec G4R 3R1. Moisie River, helicopter from Sept-iles. Freezer, washers, dryers, ice dispensers, electricity.

Sandy Annanack, 8102 Route Trans-Canada, Saint-Laurent, Quebec H4S 1R4. 514-332-0880. Chutes Helene George River, Route 138 to Sept-iles and by plane via

Schefferville. Rowboat, motors, freezer, washers, ice dispensers, electricity, services of a guide.

Auberge de la Riviere George Inc., 4 Place du Manoir, Lac-Delage, Quebec G0A 4P0. 418-585-3477. George River, seaplane via Schefferville. Canoes, rowboat, motors, life jacket, ice dispensers, electricity, hunting and fishing licenses, services of a guide, temporary shelters.

Airgava Limitee, C.P. 280, Schefferville, Quebec G0G 2T0. 418-585-2605. George River, seaplane via Schefferville. Canoes, rowboat, freezer, washers, dryers, electricity, hunting and fishing licenses, services of a guide, temporary shelters.

Club de Chasse et Peche Montagnais (1980) Inc., C.P. 489, Schefferville, Quebec G0G 2T0. 418-585-2228/627-4165. Lac alaise, seaplane via Schefferville. Canoes, rowboat, motors, life jacket, freezer, electricity, hunting and fishing licenses, services of a guide, temporary shelters.

Johnny May, Kuujjuaq, Quebec J0M 1C0. 819-964-2873. (Radio telephone via Alma) George River, seaplane via Schefferville. Canoes, rowboat, motors, washers, electricity, hunting and fishing licenses, services of a guide.

Payne Bay Fishermen & Cooperative Association, 8012 Route Trans-Canada, Saint-Laurent, Quebec H4S 1R4. 514-332-0880. Arnaud River, seaplane via Schefferville. Rowboat, motors, life jacket, freezer, washers, ice dispensers, electricity, hunting and fishing licenses, services of a guide, platform tents.

Club de Chasse et Peche Tuktu Inc., C.P. 427, Ancienne-Lorette, Quebec G2E 4W6. 418-872-3839. George River, seaplane via Schefferville. Rowboat, motors, life jacket, freezer, washers, dryers, electricity, hunting and fishing licenses, services of a guide, platform tents, temporary shelters.

Camp des Rivieres Jumelles Ltee, C.P. 572, Station K, Montreal, Quebec H1N 3R2. 514-254-6159. George River, seaplane via Schefferville. Canoes, rowboat, motors, life jacket, electricity, hunting and fishing licenses, services of a guide, temporary shelters.

Stanley Karboski, Parish, NY 13131. 315-625-7277. Whale River, seaplane via Schefferville. Canoes, motors, life jacket, freezer, electricity, hunting and fishing licenses, services of a guide, platform tents.

Whale River Salmon Camp, Pourvoyeurs Inuit et Indiens du Quebec, 2525 rue Watt, local 12, Ste-Foy, Quebec G1P 3T2. 418-659-6009. Whale River, plane via Schefferville. Pleasure boats, canoes, rowboat, motors, life jacket, freezer, electricity, hunting and fishing licenses, services of a guide, temporary shelters.

Pourvoyeurs de la Riviere Delay Inc., C.P. 1540, Schefferville, Quebec G0G 2T0. 418-585-3475/585-3775. Schefferville (Delay River), plane via Schefferville. Canoes, rowboat, motors, life jacket, freezer, washers, dryers, electricity, services of a guide, platform tents, temporary shelters.

Stanley Annanack, Kangiqsualujjuaq, Quebec J0M 1N0. 514-332-0880. Baie de Keglo, Route 138 to Sept-iles and by plane. Rowboat, motors, life jacket, freezer, electricity, services of a guide.

Rosaire Delisle Pourvoyeur Inc., 40 2e avenue ouest, La Sarre, Quebec J9Z 1E1. 819-333-4624. Garneau Lake, plane via Matagami. Canoes, rowboat, motors, life jacket, freezer, washers, dryers, ice dispensers, electricity, services of a guide.

Camp Puunik Camp Enr., C.P. 36, Kuujjuaq, Quebec J0M 1C0. 819-964-2662. Whale River, by plane to Kuujjuaq and by seaplane to the outfitter. Canoes, motors, temporary shelters.

18

The State of Salmon Today

There are so many factors and forces applied to the salmon fishing picture today that making a valid statement about the future of sport angling is risky. The problems facing the Atlantic salmon on a worldwide basis have always revolved around one central fact: Atlantic salmon are good to eat. Their flesh has long fetched a premium price in the marketplace and will continue to do so. For many years the netting of Atlantics was largely a river-mouth operation. Since the salmon return unerringly to the rivers of their birth, the commercial fishermen knew precisely when and where the silver bounty would show up each year. Netting fish at the entrances to rivers was relatively easy, and for the century between 1850 and 1950, the demand for fresh salmon was met with enough fish escaping the mesh to provide rod and reel anglers with adequate sport. Then, in the 1950s it was discovered that the majority of Atlantic salmon journeyed to a feeding ground in the Davis Strait off the west coast of Greenland. This cold arctic water, rich with capelin and prawns, drew salmon from North America, Europe, and the British Isles. Only the salmon native to Iceland didn't visit the spot. They seemed to stay quite close to their island for winter feeding.

Practically every fishing fleet in the world made trips to the Davis Strait during the sixties and seventies in a wild rush to cash in on the salmon bonanza. It has been well recorded in many books and periodicals that the salmon stocks of the world dropped drastically over a fifteen-year span. They dropped in such a hurry that some rivers went from offering excellent fishing to *no* fishing in one year.

The ups and downs (mostly downs) of salmon stocks around the world have been diligently recorded in the pages of the *Atlantic Salmon Journal,* the quarterly magazine of the Atlantic Salmon Federation. More than any other organization, this group has fought the good fight and strived to bring reason to a highly complex issue—much too complex to address in depth in a book about angling for Atlantic salmon, but I can't resist the opportunity to make some personal observations.

Since Canada has the lion's share of quality salmon fishing today, it follows that they have the most to gain or lose in the quest to maintain an adequate salmon sport fishery. The trick is how to do this and also keep a commercial fishery intact. If we look at the "business" of Atlantic salmon, there is no question about where the money is. On some rivers a fish caught on rod and reel is worth more than a hundred dollars per pound. Even that figure would be low for many visiting anglers. Consider a round-trip air ticket from St. Louis to Quebec, say, at five hundred dollars, and a week at a salmon camp at fifteen hundred; forget any incidental expenses (and there are always a lot of them). A two-thousand-dollar price tag would mean two ten-pound fish, or four five-pounders, to reach the hundred-dollar-per-pound figure. The majority of tourist salmon anglers don't catch two ten-pounders per trip. On some rivers, the angler might do better, but realistically many salmon trips produce exactly zero. Therefore, the average price per pound can be much higher than a hundred dollars. At commercial fish counters, fresh Atlantic salmon ranged from fourteen dollars per pound to nearly twice that in 1986. I have no doubt all prices will go higher in the future.

The sport anglers and the commercial fishermen from all nations have had a nasty past, arguing, badgering, and engaging in some direct physical contact over the years. Canadian newspapers have printed dozens of stories telling the "Yankees" to keep their noses out of Canadian affairs, and in return the U.S. salmon angler, who must visit Canada if he is to enjoy salmon fishing, has blasted the Canadian commercial fishermen as some breed of near caveman whose mission in life is to kill the last salmon on earth. As with all such heated issues, the facts soon become obscured in rhetoric with little of value being accomplished.

This bad state of affairs began to change about twenty years ago, when some U.S. anglers finally realized that Canadian commercial fishermen had a legitimate gripe. The argument that commercial salmon fishing was hurting sport fishing was true enough and few denied it, but it was also true that a fair amount of salmon netting could be done without hurting the parent stocks. But far beyond these economic and biological issues were the deeply rooted traditions of gathering food from the sea. The maritime provinces of Canada have long been inhabited by a rugged breed of sailors and self-sustaining woodspeople who discovered how to survive without much help from any government agency. Times may change quickly, but people don't. It's a shocking blow for a hard-working son-of-the-sea to be told that netting salmon must be curtailed or even stopped on some waters. When a man's family has been setting gill nets and purse seines since their recorded history began in the 1600s, not doing so is unthinkable. Money aside, it's what certain families have always done. The greater part of their livelihoods might well come from other endeavors, but salmon netting is in the blood, and the local Canadian politician who overlooks this could be in serious trouble. Again, the Atlantic Salmon Federation, with its international membership and officers, mostly Canadian and U.S., kept trying to find some middle ground to convince both sides to examine the other's position. I think it's happening today, and with far better effect than many observers expected.

At considerable expense, commercial salmon fishing licenses are being bought by the provinces, and no new licenses are being issued. The daily and season limits for sport anglers have been reduced in all provinces over the past ten years, and catch and release programs have been instituted. In New Brunswick, Nova Scotia, Prince Edward Island, and Newfoundland, the taking of adult salmon has been temporarily banned and the season limits for anglers pegged at low figures–grilse only, with all salmon more than twenty-five inches long to be released.

To those not familiar with the individuality of salmon rivers or the natural history of the fish, killing the small fish and returning the larger ones may seem odd. It's perfectly understandable when we consider that grilse beget grilse and large salmon beget large salmon. It's in the genes for a fish to feed more than one season in the salt water. Some stay in the ocean two, three, four, and even five years before returning to their natal river. In doing so, they become large fish, which is what both commercial and sport fishermen are seeking. Big fish are stronger, able to overcome greater obstacles and adversity, and they are healthier. They also produce more and larger eggs, which in turn have a greater chance of survival. Until we reach the point where our salmon rivers are once again producing the maximum-size fish they're capable of, releasing most of the adult fish we catch is good business.

The tagging of individual fish by sport and commercial fishermen in the salmon fishing provinces of Canada has also helped keep score on who's doing what. Bartering or selling an untagged fish is a violation of the law. When your tags are used up, you're done. This move also encourages catch and release.

Convincing some guides and not a few sports that releasing a salmon was a wise thing to do did not come about easily. Many fishermen thought that spent salmon, because of their violent leaps, slashing runs, and heroic struggles, were sure to die. Why release a fish that was already doomed? To his everlasting credit, Lee Wulff was advocating the release of large salmon more than forty years ago. With his vast salmon fishing experience, including the pioneering of salmon angling as a business in New-

A blue plastic tag must be attached to all salmon in Quebec before they are transported from the river. This is the case in most Canadian provinces today, and the legal quota of salmon tags are issued with each license and numbered accordingly.

foundland, Lee proved to his own satisfaction that salmon could survive if played well and not handled too much. By placing caught salmon in riverside enclosures and small brooks, Lee convinced many skeptics that they didn't all die. For perhaps a hundred years, Eskimos of the Ungava Bay region of Quebec kept salmon alive for months in small holding dams until they were eaten.

With the passage of the Anadromous Fish and Conservation Act of 1965, the restoration of Atlantic salmon to their traditional home rivers of New England began in earnest. The Connecticut River, once the greatest salmon river in North America, was devoid of this fish as early as 1815. Dams and industrial pollution had done the job quickly. We were proficient at water quality destruction even then. Atlantic salmon have not yet reached fishable populations in the Connecticut and its tributaries, but I honestly believe that day is not far off.

Salmon have been nicely restored to a number of Maine rivers, and more man-hours of salmon angling take place there every year. Although there are some minor ups and downs in yearly counts, the overall trend is upward in numbers of fish taken by rod and reel. The Merrimack River in Massachusetts is also receiving attention, and more than two hundred fish arrived at the Essex Fish Lift near Lawrence last year. Even Rhode Island is getting in on the act with plantings of juvenile salmon in the Pawcatuck River. We are learning and we are trying.

I am highly optimistic about the future of the Atlantic salmon. Frankly, I wasn't so sure some twenty or even ten years ago. It appeared that a combination of high seas netters from a dozen nations, the greed at the river mouths, the poaching bandits, indifferent governments, and a lack of unity among sport fishermen spelled the end of this great fish. Most of us who write about such things felt this way. It is getting better.

On several rivers fished during the past half dozen years, I've seen fish return in greater numbers and a small but steady increase in the overall size of the average salmon. We cannot, however, ease up on carrying the banner of restoration. Without constant goading, plans and programs have a way of stalling, and new threats such as acid rain and industrial accidents are constantly presenting new obstacles. The effort is worth it, no matter how great the challenges seem at times. To have an abundance of the Atlantic Ocean's finest and most mysterious game fish is to preserve a global treasure. (For information about joining the Atlantic Salmon Federation, write to: ASF, 1435 St. Alexandre, Suite 1030, Montreal, Quebec, Canada H3A 2G4.)

To those who do not fish and particularly to those who have not seen or felt an Atlantic salmon on the end of their leaders, it must seem curious that such passion be held for such a small-brained creature. Try as we do to be eloquent in praising the Atlantic salmon, our words frequently fall on deaf ears. While it's true the salmon is but one species in the vast cornucopia of aquatic life, it's a nearly perfect gauge of water quality in its twin homes, the freshwater rivers and the saltwater ocean, and of human stewardship of our natural resources. If the salmon can't survive, can we?

Index

Adams dry fly, 150
Adult salmon, definition of, 19
AFTMA (American Fishing Tackle Manufacturers
  Association), 76
Albright knot, 77, 84
Alcott, Ron, 138
Alevin stage of development, 14
American Fly Tyer, The, 137
American shad/shad fishing, Atlantic salmon/salmon
  fishing compared to, 48
Anadromous Fish and Conservation Act of 1965,
  217
Angler's and Shooter's Bookshelf, 135
Atlantic Salmon Federation, 214, 215, 217
Atlantic Salmon Journal, The, 214

Bashline, Sylvia, 29, 47–48, 68, 180, 181
Bass/bass fishing, Atlantic salmon/salmon fishing
  compared to, 132, 162, 172
Bates, Joseph D., Jr., 136
Bathtub Rock, 27, 29, 31
Belle Isle, Strait of, 132
Benchill fly, 149
Berkley lines, 76
Berners, Dame Juliana, 129
Billy Pate reel, 74
Black Bear flies
    Blue Charm, 44, 46, 124, 133, 138, 142, 149
    Green-Butt, 124, 133, 149
    Red-Butt (Conrad), 46–47, 122, 124, 149
    Thunder and Lightning, 124, 138, 146, 149

Black Bivisibles, 150
Black Doctor fly, 142, 149
Black Dose fly, 149, 155
Black flies, list of, 149
Blackmoor's Pool, 40–41, 43–44, 46
Black Rat fly, 133, 149
Black salmon (kelts), 14
Black spiders, 150
Black Woodchuck fly, 149
Blue Charm fly, 44, 46, 124, 133, 138, 142, 149
Blue Doctor fly, 142, 149
Blue flies, list of, 149
Blue Rat fly, 149
Bobbitt, Eldon, 50, 52, 133
    Eldon Special fly of, 127, 133
Bogdan, Stanley, 70
Bodgan reels
    Ross, 70
    S-2, 70
Bomber (Cigar-Butt, or Shaggy Rat) fly, 133, 146,
  148, 150, 158
    fishing with a, 159–62
Bonefish/bonefish fishing, Atlantic salmon/salmon
  fishing compared to, 48, 166
Borders, Larry, 137
Boyd, Megan, 137
Britain, 144, 145, 154, 213
Brown Bivisibles, 150
Brown spiders, 150
Buck Bugs flies, 160–61
Butterfly fly, 133

Camp Pool One, 50, 52
Camp Pool Two, 35
Catina reel, 74
CFO series reels, 70
Chandler, Leon, 76
Char/char fishing, Atlantic salmon/salmon fishing
   compared to, 173
Cigar-Butt fly. *See* Bomber fly
Cleaning and Cooking Fish, 181
Cleaning the catch, 179–80
Clothing, 176, 178
Cock-of-the-Rock fly, 136
Colburn pattern, 127
Complete Book of Fly Tying, The, 136
Connecticut River, 217
Conrad (Red-Butt) fly, 46–47, 122, 124, 149
Cooking the catch, 180–81
Cortland Line Company, 76
     444SL line, 76
     Micron line, 77
Cortland SS Magnum reel, 70
Cosseboom fly, 133, 138, 143, 147, 149
Costs of
     a good guide, 168, 170
     salmon fishing, 173–74, 214
Crossfield fly, 142, 149
Cummins reels, 64
Curry, 47–48

Dacron line, 77
Davis Strait, 16, 213–14
Deerfield rods, 60, 61
Dee River, 144
Dee strip flies, 136, 144
Delrin, 70
Bill DeWitt Company, 175
Doak, Wally, 131–32
Doaktown, New Brunswick, 131
Double-hook flies, 150–51
Dry flies
     fishing with, 153–56, 158–62
     list of, 150
Durham Ranger fly, 137, 138, 149
Dusty Miller fly, 138, 149

Eagle River, 84, 153, 156, 158, 165–66, 172–73
     Bathtub Rock, 27, 29, 31
     junction pool with Ookpack Brook, 159–60
Echo Beach fly, 146
Egg stage of development, 14
Eldon Special fly, 127, 133
Elk Hair Caddis dry fly, 150
Ent, Bob, 137–38
Essex Fish Lift, 217
Eyeglasses, 176, 178

Farlow reels, 64

Fenwick Company
     graphite rods, 59
     model 107 rod, 58
     rods, 50, 58–59, 61
     Traditionals rods, 59
     World Class reels, 70, 74
Field & Stream, 154
Fin-Nor Tycoon reels, 74
Fisher Company, 60
Flies, 131, 135
Fly, choosing a, 123–25, 127, 129, 131–39, 141–51
Fly boxes, 175–76
Fly Tyer, 136
444SL line, 76
Fox, Charlie, 80–81
Frank's Run, 31
Fulsher, Keith, 136

Gaffing, 115
Garcia lines, 76
Gaspé Peninsula, 132, 173
General Practitioner fly, 136
George River, 143, 154–55
     chances of catching salmon in the, 173
Goins, Tommy, 35
Grand Cascapedia River, 154
Gray Bivisibles, 150
Gray dry flies, 150
Gray flies, list of, 149
Gray Rat fly, 149
Green, Jimmy, 59
Green-Butt fly, 124, 133, 149
Green flies, list of, 149
Green Highlander fly, 138, 143, 149
Greenland, 20, 213
Green Rat fly, 149
Green Woodchuck fly, 149
Grilse
     definition of, 16, 19
     fishing for, 39, 47, 57–58, 77, 88, 92, 115, 118,
        122, 156, 174, 215
Grizzly King fly, 143, 149
Gros Mecatina River. *See* Mecatina River
Groupers/grouper fishing, Atlantic salmon/salmon
     fishing compared to, 118
Guide(s), 180
     cost of a good, 168, 170
     importance of a competent, 31, 163–66
     techniques of an experienced, 94
     what to expect of a good, 166, 168

Hair-Wing Atlantic Salmon Flies, 136
Hairy Mary fly, 138
Handtailing, 94, 96
Hardy
     LRH reel, 64
     Marquis reel, 64, 68

Perfect reel, 64, 68
Prince reel, 64
reels, 64, 68, 70
rods, 58, 61
St. Aiden reel, 64
St. George reel, 64
St. John reel, 64, 68
Harry's Ledge, 31
Hathaway, Norm, 159–60, 172–73
Hats, 176
Haystack dry fly, 150, 158, 159
Helmsdale Doctor fly, 142
Herring/herring fishing, Atlantic salmon/salmon
 fishing compared to, 125
Herter's Fly Tying Manual, 135
Hill, Curt, 49, 159
 Haystack dry fly of, 150, 158, 159
Hook, choosing a, 124
How to Dress Salmon Flies, 135
How to find the best fishing spots, 27
Hunter, Bill, 138
Hunt River, 22, 96, 115, 153
 Hunt River Falls, 35

Iceland, 23, 124, 142, 144, 145, 154, 213
Improved Clinch knot, 84
Indian Crow fly, 136
Insect repellent, 178
Ireland, 144, 154, 162

Jacks/jack fishing, Atlantic salmon/salmon fishing
 compared to, 118
Jock Scott fly, 48, 133, 137, 138, 146, 147, 149
Jorgensen, Poul, 136, 137, 142

Kelson, George M., 123, 135, 138, 145–46
Kelts (black salmon), 14
Korosec, Andy, 43
Korosec, Bob, 43, 122
Krom, Charles, 136

Labrador, 19, 49
 chances of catching salmon in, 173
 Eagle River, 27, 29, 31, 84, 153, 156, 158,
  159–60, 165–66, 172–73
 general salmon fishing information, 200–202
 Hunt River, 22, 35, 96, 115, 153
 Little Minipi River, 162
 Ookpack (Owl) Brook, 159–60
 Sandhill River, 146–47
Labrador Bugs flies, 160–61
Lawrence, Massachusetts, 217
Leaders, choosing, 79–81, 84, 86
Leadwing Coachman pattern, 144
Leiser, Eric, 136
Leonard, J. Edson, 131, 135
Leonard rods, 61

Letort brown, 158
Limerick bend hook, 161
Lines, choosing, 75–77
Little Minipi River, 162
Little Southwest Miramichi River, 20, 188
 Blackmoor's Pool, 40–41, 43–44, 46
 Oxbow Pool, 41, 43, 46–47
 Red Stone Pool, 80–81
Loomis rods, 61
LRH reel, 64

MacPherson, Maxwell, Jr., 138
Maine, 19, 127, 160, 217
 Penobscot River, 144
Main Southwest Miramichi River, 16, 77, 131, 188
 chances of catching salmon in the, 171
Margaree River, 144, 185
Marinaro, Vince, 64, 144
Maritime provinces, 23, 81, 131, 214–15
Marlin/marlin fishing, Atlantic salmon/salmon
 fishing compared to, 120
Mar Lodge fly, 148
Marquis reel, 64, 68
Martin MG-9 reel, 70
Massachusetts
 Essex Fish Lift, 217
 Lawrence, 217
 Merrimack River, 217
Matane, Quebec, 118
Matchett, Earl, 41, 43, 165
Maxima monofilament, 81
Mecatina River, 87, 132–33
 Camp Pool One, 50, 52
 Camp Pool Two, 35
 Sidewalk Pool, 161
 Snakepit Pool, 147
 Steady Pool, 29, 31, 47–48, 68
Medalist reels
 model 1494, 68
 model 1495, 68
 model 1495½, 68
 model 1498, 68
Merrimack River, 217
Micron line, 77
Miramichi River. *See* Little Southwest Miramichi
 River; Main Southwest Miramichi River;
 Northwest Miramichi River
A Modern Dry Fly Code, 144
Moisie River, 146
Muddler Minnow fly, 143, 155, 158
Muskie/muskie fishing, Atlantic salmon/salmon
 fishing compared to, 132
Mustad hooks, 124

New Brunswick, 19, 153, 163
 best rivers, list of, 188–89
 chances of catching salmon in, 173

Doaktown, 131
fishing outfitters, list of, 189–99
general salmon fishing information, 187–88
Little Southwest Miramichi River, 20, 40–41, 43–44, 46–47, 80–81, 188
Main Southwest Miramichi River, 16, 77, 131, 171, 188, 189
Northwest Miramichi River, 165, 188
Red Bank, 20, 40, 41
Silliker, 40
temporary ban on taking of adult salmon, 215
New England, 134, 138, 217
Newfoundland, 19, 49, 163, 215, 217
chances of catching salmon in, 173
fishing outfitters, list of, 202–8
general salmon fishing information, 200–202
temporary ban on taking of adult salmon, 215
See also Labrador
Newfoundland and Labrador Hunting and Fishing, 202
Night Hawk fly, 125, 148
North Shore area, St. Lawrence River, 173
Northwest Miramichi River, 165, 188
Norway, 174
Nova Scotia
best rivers, list of, 184–85
fishing outfitters, list of, 186–87
general salmon fishing information, 183–84, 185
Margaree River, 144, 185
temporary ban on taking of adult salmon, 215
Nuevo Quebec, 173

Ookpack (Owl) Brook, 159–60
Orange Parson fly, 146
Orvis, 61
CFO series reels, 70
graphite rods, 59–60
multipiece rods, 60
Presentation reel, 70
SSS floating line, 76
Outdoor Life, 49
Owl (Ookpack) Brook, 159–60
Oxbow Pool, 41, 43, 46–47

Pacific salmon/salmon fishing, Atlantic salmon/salmon fishing compared to, 13
Paor, Peter, 29
Parr stage of development, 14
feeding habits of parr, 156, 158
Partridge hooks, 124
Pawcatuck River, 217
Penobscot River, 144
Perfect reel, 64, 68
Permit/permit fishing, Atlantic salmon/salmon fishing compared to, 48
Pfeiffer, Boyd, 178
Pflueger, Medalist reels of, 68
Photographing the fish, 94, 96, 115

Pierce, Carol, 161
Pike/pike fishing, Atlantic salmon/salmon fishing compared to, 162
Portland Hitch (Riffle Hitch), 49, 84, 124, 146
Presentation reel, 70
Prince Edward Island
general salmon fishing information, 199–200
temporary ban on taking of adult salmon, 215
Prince reel, 64
Pryce-Tannatt, Thomas Edwin, 135, 138, 139

Quebec, 133, 173
chances of catching salmon in, 173
fishing outfitters, list of, 208–12
Gaspé Peninsula, 132, 173
George River, 143, 154–55
Matane, 118
Mecatina River, 29, 31, 35, 47–48, 50, 52, 68, 132–33, 147, 161
Moisie River, 146
North Shore area, 173
Nuevo Quebec, 173
St. Lawrence River, 19, 29, 146, 173
Ungava Bay, 19, 143, 154, 173, 217
Whale River, 173

Randall, Dave, 132–33
Red Ball waders, 176
Red Bank, New Brunswick, 20, 40, 41
Red-Butt (Conrad) fly, 46–47, 122, 124, 149
Red Stone Pool, 80–81
Reel, choosing a, 63–64, 68, 70
Rhode Island, Pawcatuck River of, 217
Riffle Hitch (Portland Hitch), 49, 84, 124, 146
Rod, choosing a, 53–61
Ross reel, 70
Royal Coachman fly, 144
Royal dry flies, 150
Rusty Rat fly, 48, 133, 138, 149

Sage, 61
multipiece rods, 60
St. Aiden reel, 64
St. Croix rods, 61
St. George reel, 64
St. John reel, 64, 68
St. Lawrence River, 19, 29, 146
North Shore area of the, 173
Salmon Flies, 136, 142, 145
Salmon Fly, The, 135
Samson, Jack, 154–55
Sandhill River, 146–47
Scientific Anglers (SA)
lines, 76
"System" rods, 58
System II Model 8/9 reel, 70

Scotland, 162
    Dee River, 144
    Sneezort River, 49
    Spey River, 144
Seamaster reel, 74
Shad/shad fishing, Atlantic salmon/salmon fishing
    compared to, 125
Shaggy Rat fly. *See* Bomber fly
Shakespeare
    lines, 76, 176
    rods, 61
Sharks/shark fishing, Atlantic salmon/salmon fishing
    compared to, 118, 120
Shaw, Helen, 136
Sidewalk Pool, 161
Silliker, Guy, 43
Silliker, New Brunswick, 40
Silver Blue fly, 142
Silver-bodied flies, list of, 148
Silver Doctor fly, 125, 127, 137, 142, 146, 148, 149
Silver Gray fly, 149
Silver Monkey wing, 149–50
Silver Rat fly, 127, 133, 146, 148
Silver Wilkinson fly, 148
Skyline rods, 61
Smith, Ned, 46–47
Smolt stage of development, 14, 16
Snakepit Pool, 147
Sneezort River, 49
Snowball, Conluci, 154
Sonny, 96
Spey flies, 144
Spey River, 144
SSS floating line, 76
Steady Pool, 29, 31, 47–48, 68
S-2 reel, 70
Sunglasses, 176
Surface Stone Fly, 159
Swordfish/swordfish fishing, Atlantic salmon/salmon
    fishing compared to, 120
Sylvester, Dave, 60
"System" rods, 58
System II Model 8/9 reel, 70

Tarpon/tarpon fishing, Atlantic salmon/salmon
    fishing compared to, 48

Ted Williams fly, 160–61
Thomas & Thomas (T & T), 61
    bamboo rods, 59
    graphite rods, 59
    multipiece rods, 60
3M Company, 76
Thunder and Lightning fly, 124, 138, 146, 149
Tiemco hooks, 124
Traditionals rods, 59
Triangle Taper line, 77
Trout/trout fishing, Atlantic salmon/salmon fishing
    compared to, 132, 156, 162, 172
Tuna/tuna fishing, Atlantic salmon/salmon fishing
    compared to, 118, 120
Turle knot, 84
Tycoon reels, 74
Tying Flies, 136

Ungava Bay, 19, 143, 154, 173, 217

Vests, 176

Waders, 176
Wading staff, 176
Walker, Alf, 137
Walleye/walleye fishing, Atlantic salmon/salmon
    fishing compared to, 132, 166
Western steelhead/steelhead fishing, Atlantic
    salmon/salmon fishing compared to, 48, 77
Whale River, 173
Wheatley fly boxes, 175–76
White dry flies, 150
White spiders, 150
Whitlock, Dave, 136
Williams, Ted, 160
Wilson Dry Fly Hook, 150
Wise, Jack, 96, 115
World Class reels, 70, 74
Wulff, Lee, 16, 49, 53, 135, 215, 217
    dry flies of, 150, 158, 159
    Triangle Taper line of, 77

Young, J. W., reels, 64